John Osborne

FOUR PLAYS

A SENSE OF DETACHMENT
THE END OF ME OLD CIGAR
JILL AND JACK
A PLACE CALLING ITSELF ROME

OBERON BOOKS
LONDON

A Sense of Detachment and *A Place Calling Itself Rome* first
published in 1973, *The End of Me Old Cigar* and *Jill and Jack* first
published in 1975, all four by Faber and Faber Ltd.

First published in this edition in 2000 by Oberon Books Ltd.
(incorporating Absolute Classics)
521 Caledonian Road, London N7 9RH
Tel: 020 7607 3637 / Fax: 020 7607 3629
e-mail: oberon.books@btinternet.com

A catalogue record for this book is available from the British
Library.

ISBN: 1 84002 074 1

Cover photograph: Every effort has been made to obtain
permission to use this picture.

Typography: Richard Doust

Printed in Great Britain by Antony Rowe Ltd, Reading.

Contents

INTRODUCTION

A Sense of Detachment
The End of Me Old Cigar
Jill and Jack

Helen Osborne

These plays were written in the early 1970s and, contrary to hearsay-history, very dispiriting years they were. With Heath and Wilson as regnant Gauleiters, the miners struck, the lights went out and the Three-Day week came in. Everyone felt miffed.

The infant Women's Movement not only had a toe in the door but its knees under the table and a knife up its knickers. In the theatre the gleeful celebrations at the long overdue removal of the Lord Chamberlain's blue pencil had deteriorated into a manic free-for-all. The harmony of language was an early victim. Stuck for an image? Shove in a 'shit' or a 'screw'. 'Audience Participation' was the buzz. 'Happenings' were hip. No use sitting there with a box of chocs when a hairy actor might crash into your lap. Get up. Join in. And never mind the B.O.

It was not a time for meticulous or passionate wordsmiths. But behind his redoubt, Osborne watched and listened. *A Sense of Detachment* was his first salvo, and he flipped the futilities of the 'Theatre of Antagonism' – accompanied by its smug 'device of insult' – upside down.

How the critics hated it, their mimsy, dumpy noses twitching at this rank abuse of an already incipient Political Correctness. Not only the jokes but the 'joke' itself blithely passed them by. They were right behind the Girl when she declares, 'He really has got a bit too predicable now, hasn't he?'

But not too predictable for some of the punters. 'I suppose it's all really about things like music and fucking,' said Rachel Kempson's Older Lady as, with crystal elocution, she waded through a pile of ever-more explicit porn catalogues.

One evening, a woman in the audience threw her boot at Lady Redgrave, who hurled it back. This was no 'device'.

The word went out that subversive anarchy, the genuine article, was happily rampant once again in Sloane Square and the limited run quickly sold out. There was a spontaneous party for 'S' of 'D' fans, led by the cast, on the Royal Court stage. We danced and sang and then whooped off into the night and illicit liaisons. The play made you feel young, cheeky, unfashionably enthusiastic – about undying poetry, romantic music, the tender mystery of love between men and women – and *really* liberated. Although, as the Chap reminded us, 'It's only a vision.'

This is a true piece of theatre. It wouldn't transfer to film or television. Even the stage directions could only have been written by an actor… ('As the audience returns, if indeed it does return…'). Pure John Osborne.

You only have to read *A Better Class of Person*, his first volume of autobiography, to realise how much he plundered his inner life in *A Sense of Detachment*, how personal it was to him, this stylised threnody to the loss and erosion of English character, genius and gentleness by a concerted and strident coarsening. 'Woman is dead! Long live woman!' cries the Chap. And then, 'I do not believe it. She has always triumphed in my small corner of spirit. Being in love! What anathema to the Sexual Militant!'

The same oblique 'vision' feeds *The End of Me Old Cigar*, with its conventional County House Weekend setting which disguises a Garsington of lechery, and much besides. Regine, the Madame of this militant bordello, and her Amazon troop of call-girls, are working up to Bastille Day when they will blow up not only the reputations of their famous clients but the very notion of '*Man*kind'.

'Remember,' says Regine, when issuing her battle directives, 'it's the last time over that timeless top and then a New World waits for us.' The Sisters are assured they are about to 're-enter Paradise. On our own terms.' But hormones and heartbeats are stronger than propaganda, and messy old love gets in the way, as it always will.

At this distance, what I find most moving about these plays, along with their unique voice, their fun and larkiness, is the use of music: Mozart, Mahler's Fifth, Vaughan Williams, Elgar, Handel, 'Rosenkavalier,' which would become so familiar, day by day, when John and I were married. Snatches from the Music Hall, of course…and Osborne's soupy old favourites like 'In a Little Gypsy Tearoom' or 'I'm Only a Strolling Vagabond.' Gone, but not quite forgotten.

Helen Osborne
Shropshire, 2000

A SENSE OF DETACHMENT

GRANDFATHER: I suppose all life is a theatre.

CHAP: And all theatre is *laife*.

GIRL: What a profound insight!

CHAP: You mean *obvious*?

GIRL: Naturally.

INTERRUPTER: Is it all going to be as formless as this?

CHAIRMAN: Yes.

CHAP: I expect so.

GIRL: *You* try learning the bloody stuff. I've forgotten half of it already.

INTERRUPTER:(*From the stalls.*) You're trying to have it all ways, aren't you?

GIRL: As the actress said to the bishop.

INTERRUPTER: Do you think we can't see through this?

GRANDFATHER: I shouldn't think *he'll* sit through it.

GIRL: He will.

CHAP: We know, he's paid for it.

CHAIRMAN: Yes, I think we've had enough of him for a bit, don't you?

CHAP: Bit of your old Pirandello, like.

CHAIRMAN: (*To the INTERRUPTER.*) Yes, I should go to the bar and have a drink.

GIRL: Don't think the Management will pay for it!

CHAP: I suppose *that's* a character trait, is it?

GIRL: What?

CHAIRMAN: Well, I suppose we'd better make some sort of start, though I don't know why.

GIRL: You either freeze to death or boil your knickers off.

INTERRUPTER: (*Walking out of the auditorium.*) Bloody right! Load of rubbish!

CHAP: (*In a pompous voice.*) Hear, hear!

INTERRUPTER: My small boy could do better than this.

CHAP: Yes, I bet he likes small boys an' all.

(*NOTE: If there are any genuine interruptions from members of the audience at any time, and it would be a pity if there were not, the actors must naturally be prepared to deal with such a situation, preferably the CHAIRMAN, the CHAP or the GIRL. These can be obvious, inventive or spontaneous,*

*apart from the obvious responses like 'Piss off', 'Get knotted',
'Go and fuck yourself if you can get it up, which I doubt from
the look of you', etc.*

*These could be adapted to the appearance or apparent
background, like:*

'Get back off to the shires, you married pouf,'

'If you're Irish, get out of the parlour.'

'And I hope the ship goes dozen in Galway Bay.'

'Get back to Golders Green, you hairy git.'

*'Why aren't you in the West End, watching some old tatty
expensive shit?'*

*The INTERRUPTER can return at any of these with any of
the following abusive lines:*

'What we want is family entertainment.'

*'When you've had a hard day's work, you don't want to sit
and listen to a lot of pseudo-intellectual filth.'*

'Bourgeois crap.'

*'Do you expect to get the young people into the theatre this
way?'*

'Who cares about them? What about us?'

'All too obvious, I'm afraid.'

'Like it doesn't do anything for me, man.'

'I hope that the women are being paid the same as the men.'

'Like what's it all for, man?'

'They did all this in the 1930s, only better.'

'I'm glad I haven't got any money in the show.'

And so on.)

CHAIRMAN: Now where were we?

GIRL: Nowhere.

CHAP: Absobloodylutely nowhere.

(*From the loudspeakers comes the lush sound of the Adagietto
from Mahler's 'Fifth'. They all listen in silence for a while.*)

CHAIRMAN: Oh, I don't think we need *that*, do you?

CHAP: I don't know, I should think we probably do.

CHAIRMAN: Always used to sneer at it, I remember.

GIRL: Still do, some of them.

OLDER LADY: Rather good ballet music, don't you think?

CHAIRMAN: Oh Christ! (*To the CHAP.*) Anyway, ask him
   to turn it down, will you?

FATHER: I can do a passable Melville Gideon.

GRANDFATHER: Now he really *was* good.

GIRL: Don't start yet.

CHAP: I like barrel organs.

CHAIRMAN: Yes, I know what you mean.

GIRL: Oh, do get on with it!

CHAP: (*To the CHAIRMAN.*) Yes, you *are* the Chairman and she wants her pay packet.

GIRL: I'm just thinking about what I'm going to have to eat afterwards.

CHAIRMAN: Why should *I* be the Chairman?

CHAP: You know perfectly well.

GIRL: Yes.

CHAP: You're the best equipped academically, apart from which you're a brilliant promotionalist, an eyes upward grown-in Committee Man.

OLDER LADY: Very good actor too.

GIRL: What do you mean, good actor? He's a bloody amateur. Always has been. That's why people think he's so good.

CHAP: That's why he thinks he's so good too.

CHAIRMAN: (*Rising.*) Well, if you're going to be like that...

CHAP: Of course we're going to be like that.

GIRL: Oh yes, don't be *faux naif.* Just get *on* with it.

CHAP: Oh, is that how you pronounce it?

GIRL: What?

CHAP: *Faux naif,* you avaricious little berk.

CHAIRMAN: *Right,* we'll start.

GIRL: Thank God for that. I'm hungry already.

CHAP: You would be.

CHAIRMAN: (*Addressing the audience.*) Er...

GIRL: Ladies and gentlemen!

CHAP: *That* lot?

CHAIRMAN: What else do I call them?

GIRL: Who cares?

CHAP: Perhaps some of them *are* ladies and gentlemen.

GIRL: I doubt it.

CHAIRMAN: Try not to be too censorious.

GIRL: I don't know what that means.

CHAP: Bitchy.

CHAIRMAN: (*Addressing the audience again.*) *Some* ladies and gentlemen and the rest...
(*There is an enormous commotion as the MAN IN THE STAGE BOX stumbles in noisily, looks around at the stage and leers drunkenly at the audience. He is wearing an enormous fake fur coat, a striped football scarf and cap.*)

BOX MAN: What's all this then?

CHAIRMAN: (*Burying his face in his hands.*) Oh no, not that old one!

CHAP: Yes, running short I'd say.

BOX MAN: Running short? *We've* been running short – all the brown ale we've had. Up Chelsea!

CHAP: And up you too!

GIRL: I never understand these gags. Exclusively male, I suppose.

CHAP: (*In mock imitation of her.*) Oh yes, I dare say that's *very* true. *Very* true. Exclusively male.

BOX MAN: What's *she* then? Women's Lib? (*He snorts at his own joke.*)

GIRL: I knew it was a mistake.

BOX MAN: It's a bloody mistake all right. Your mother's mistake!

GIRL: (*To the CHAIRMAN.*) Such an amusing theatrical device.

BOX MAN: I'M IN THE WRONG BLEEDING THEATRE!

CHAIRMAN: We're all in the wrong bleeding theatre.

BOX MAN: Is this Drury Lane?

GIRL: No, and it's not *Fiddler on the Roof* either.

OLDER LADY: What did he say?

BOX MAN: *You* can drop 'em for a start!

OLDER LADY: I suppose you think I wouldn't?

BOX MAN: All right, don't bother. Is there a change of scenery?

CHAIRMAN: No, but I'm afraid there will probably be some music.

GIRL: If you can call a barrel organ music.

BOX MAN: Go on, Grandad, give us a tune!

GRANDFATHER: No respect left.

OLDER LADY: Why should they?

BOX MAN: I can't make head or tail of this lot.

GIRL: And you won't. No tits.

CHAP: Oh, he's not such a bad idea.

BOX MAN: (*Standing up and addressing the audience.*) Well, if you're going to fuck the chicken, I'll dangle my balls in the pink blancmange.

GIRL: Now what's he talking about?

CHAP: Does it matter?

(*The INTERRUPTER enters from dress circle.*)

INTERRUPTER: Rubbish! I want my money back.

BOX MAN: Yes, well I'm going to go and have a slash.

GIRL: Yes, we know, after all that brown ale.

BOX MAN: Oh, I could do something for you, Daisy.

GIRL: My name's not Daisy and *you* couldn't.

(*The INTERRUPTER disappears. The GRANDFATHER gets up slowly and plays the barrel organ gravely. The BOX MAN joins in with the song and encourages the audience to join him.*)

BOX MAN: (*Singing.*) I don't care who you are
Make yourself at home
Put your feet on the mantelshelf
Draw up a dolly and help yourself.

GRANDFATHER: (*Addressing the BOX MAN.*) Those are not the words.

BOX MAN: Well, you don't have to be like *that*! I've paid my money, haven't I?

GIRL: No.

BOX MAN: Listen, you don't have to get all toffee-nosed with *me*. Or any of these other good people. We *make* you, the likes of you. Mr John Public, that's what we are. Mr and Mrs John Public.

GIRL: I hope you'll be very happy together.

BOX MAN: We are – what's wrong with that I'd like to know? It's all right for you lot, sitting down there, looking all pleased with yourselves, getting paid hundreds of pounds.

CHAP: (*To the GIRL.*) There you are.

BOX MAN: Where would you *be*, I'd like to know –

GIRL: You're repeating yourself.

CHAP: (*To the GIRL.*) So are you.

BOX MAN: Thank you, sir. Now you're a gentleman, I can see that.

GIRL: He can't even...

BOX MAN: That's enough of *your* lip. Don't think I wouldn't come down there and smack your bottom – *and* enjoy it!

GIRL: I've no doubt, you poor old thing.

BOX MAN: All I said was he was civil and a gentleman.

GIRL: He's no more of a gentleman than you are.

CHAP: Good.

BOX MAN: Like some of these people here tonight. Look at them. Beautifully-dressed, attractive women, lot of respectable people out there, including some of your real clever ones.

GIRL: Who do you think he's talking about?

CHAIRMAN: Yes, well I think we've had enough of *that*, too.

BOX MAN: What's that?

CHAIRMAN: I suggest, sir, that you come back later.

GIRL: Oh, *no*, please!

BOX MAN: I don't care what you say, I've paid my money and I'm going out for a slash.

CHAP: Perhaps it's not such a bad idea.

(*The BOX MAN stumbles out of the stage box with a maximum of noise and so on.*)

CHAIRMAN: Shall I sit in the middle?

CHAP: Lucky Pedro, in the middle again.

GIRL: I suppose that's another joke?

CHAP: Masculine.

(*The BOX MAN returns noisily. He shouts down at actors.*)

BOX MAN: That's not funny, old man! Give yourself a kick in the pants!

CHAP: He pinched that from Peter Nichols.

CHAIRMAN: Actually, *he* pinched it from George Doonan.

BOX MAN: You're all a bloody lot of thieves and robbers!
(*He staggers out.*)

CHAIRMAN: Well, as you seem to have suggested that my
personality is best suited to imposing some order on
this chaos –

CHAP: Or chaos on this order.

GIRL: As the case may be –

CHAIRMAN: I shall try to make a beginning.

INTERRUPTER: (*From the auditorium.*) And about time, I say!

CHAIRMAN: Of sorts. Well, ladies and gentlemen and so
on. The programme first, I suppose... Overpriced, as
usual. Full of useless information. Like what part of
Buckinghamshire the actors live in, how many children
they've got, what their hobbies are and the various
undistinguished television series that they've appeared
in. On the front, there's the title.

GIRL: Awful.

CHAIRMAN: Yes, I'm afraid *that* will have to be changed.

CHAP: Too late now.

GIRL: Actually, 'Too Late Now''s not a bad title.

CHAP: It's too late all right.

GIRL: Wasn't there a song called 'Too Late Now'?

CHAP: (*In a TV chat-show voice.*) Ah yes, 'a rather
predictable exercise in somewhat facile nostalgia'.

GIRL: Oh, do stop knocking everybody. Let him get on
with it.

CHAP: You still won't get paid till Friday.

CHAIRMAN: As I was saying – what was I saying?

GIRL: The programme.

CHAIRMAN: Oh yes, well we've agreed that the title will
have to be changed.

CHAP: The author's name is far too big.

CHAIRMAN: So is the director's, come to that.

CHAP: And who cares who *presented it*? What's that – just
making a lot of phone calls, having long lunches and
getting secretaries to do all the work.

GIRL: Don't talk to me about directors. If ever there was a
bogus job, that's one all right.

CHAP: Just letting all the actors do the work, like finding where the doorknobs are, finding out what the play's about by getting up and doing it, while they tell you what a genius you are.

CHAIRMAN: I don't think that's entirely fair.

CHAP: Like doing Hamlet as a Pre-Raphaelite queen.

GRANDFATHER: I used to like the old musical comedies...

FATHER: And a good revue.

GIRL: Well, you ain't going to get it, either of you.

OLDER LADY: I quite like it when they take all their clothes off.

CHAIRMAN: I'm sorry, but shall I go on or not?
   (*The BOX MAN returns noisily.*)

BOX MAN: I suppose you went to Oxford and Cambridge.

CHAIRMAN: No, actually I was only at one of them.
   Oh, dear, I suppose one shouldn't be so rude.

BOX MAN: Toffee-nosed pouf! (*He goes out.*)

CHAIRMAN: I agree with you that I may be occasionally and unforgivably toffee-nosed, but I am not a pouf.

GIRL: Oh come off it – we all know about *you.*

CHAP: You either likes one thing or the other, that's what I always say.

BOX MAN: (*Off.*) Hear, hear!

CHAIRMAN: (*To the GIRL.*) If I may correct you, my dear –

GIRL: Oh now, he's *really* being the Chairman.

CHAIRMAN: Yes, as a matter of fact, I am, and I would point out to *you* that you are out of order.

BOX MAN: (*Off.*) Hear, hear!

CHAIRMAN: You do not 'know all about me', as you put it, neither will you do so.

CHAP: I would like to support the Chairman on that.

GIRL: You would, but we'll have a right gusher of North Sea Gas out of you and your dreary life before this is over. I know that.

BOX MAN: (*Returning.*) Do you want me to sort him out, Missus?

GIRL: No, just shut up.

CHAIRMAN: (*To the BOX MAN.*) Did you have an enjoyable slash?

BOX MAN: Are you taking the mickey?

CHAIRMAN: No, I was asking what I thought was a friendly question.

BOX MAN: Well, I tell you, doesn't half pong in there!

CHAIRMAN: Yes, well I'm afraid we've been trying to put that right for years.

BOX MAN: When I think of what ordinary working-class people like me –

GIRL: You're not working-class, you're just a loud mouth.

CHAP: As well as pissed out of your arsehole.

GRANDFATHER: Oh dear, I wish you wouldn't.

OLDER LADY: I rather enjoy the freedom of expression of these young people.

GIRL: What do you mean young – he's middle-aged!

BOX MAN: When I think of what people like us, people like us who do a real job of work, not like you, *you've* never done a job of work...

GIRL: Piss off!

BOX MAN: ...pay for their seats with their hard-earned money, and don't you use that filthy language at *me*.

GIRL: Why not?

BOX MAN: Because you're an educated woman, and you ought to bleeding well know better.

GIRL: Well, I'm not educated and I don't know any better.

CHAIRMAN: (*To the BOX MAN.*) I think you've made your point, sir.

BOX MAN: Sing us a song! Oh Christ, I've got to go back to that stinking hellhole again! (*He blunders out.*)

CHAP: (*Sings.*) 'Oh God our help in ages past,
Our hope for years to come,
Our shelter from the stormy blast
(*ALL join in.*)
And our eternal home.'

GIRL: Hymns!

CHAP: Sort of scraping the barrel.

CHAIRMAN: To get back to the agenda, if that's what you can call it – I think we have dealt or at least spent enough time on this dull programme, the cupidity of the author and director –

CHAP: (*At the GIRL.*) And the actors.

CHAIRMAN: I will only add that as you will see, or have seen, or predicted, that this neither is nor was an entertainment –

CHAP: (*In an American accent.*) Nor a significant contribution to the cultural life of Our Time.

GRANDFATHER: Try not to be too nasty about the Yankees.

CHAP: Very good to us during the war.

GIRL: Well, they won it, of course.

CHAP: Yes. Flooded us with food parcels and French letters.

GRANDFATHER: And after the war.

CHAP: That's right. Lease Lend.

GRANDFATHER: Easy to sneer.

CHAP: Quite right. At least they didn't have to 'Go In', like 'Going into Europe'.

(*Stage lights flash out and either a still or film appears on the projection screen of Mr Edward Heath, smiling and waving to the full blast of the last movement of Beethoven's 'Ninth'. They all watch in silence for a few moments, then the picture goes out and the music stops.*)

INTERRUPTER: Cheap!

CHAIRMAN: I quite agree with you, sir.

INTERRUPTER: He's doing a good job!

CHAIRMAN: I quite agree with you about the cheapness aesthetically.

(*The BOX MAN stumbles back.*)

BOX MAN: All right for him. What about the poor bloody workers!

GIRL: (*To the CHAIRMAN.*) Can't you get rid of him? I thought you were supposed to have some sort of artistic responsibility or something.

BOX MAN: (*Shouting down at the GIRL.*) You know what *you* need, don't you?

GIRL: Don't tell me, I'll guess. Not that *you* could, anyway.

BOX MAN: I'll see you later.

GIRL: Not if I can help it.

BOX MAN: Here, where's the bar?

GIRL: Just leap over the edge of the box, and it's the first crawl to your left.

CHAP: *You* should get an old prick's pension.

BOX MAN: They told me it was a musical.

CHAP: (*Sings.*) 'I'm a Yankee Doodle Dandy…'

GIRL: There he goes again.

CHAP: 'A Yankee Doodle do or die…'

(*ALL join in.*)

'A real live nephew of my Uncle Sam,

Born on the fourth of July!'

(*During this, the Stars and Stripes flutter on the projection screen.*)

INTERRUPTER: Cheap!

BOX MAN: Mocking the poor bloody American flag now.

CHAP: We *can* mock the British one if you prefer.

CHAIRMAN: No, I don't think we do, do we?

INTERRUPTER: No, we don't.

BOX MAN: What about a SONG?

(*The stage lights dim, a frozen waste appears on the projection screen to the lone soprano sound from Vaughan Williams' 'Symphonia Antarctica'.*)

I don't mean that sort of highbrow stuff.

INTERRUPTER: You don't call *that* highbrow, do you?

CHAIRMAN: No. Very middlebrow I'm afraid. (*To the CHAP.*) Ask the Stage Management, will you?

(*Projection and music stops.*)

CHAIRMAN: Right, let's sing him a song then.

(*They all line up and sing the following to the tune of 'Widdicombe Fair'.*)

ALL: Harold Pinter, Harold Pinter,

Lend me your grey mare,

All along, down along, out along lea,

For I want to go to

Printing House Square,

With Arnold Wesker,

David Storey,

Edward Albee,

Must get in an American,

Charles Wood,

Charlie Farnsbarns,

Christopher Hampton,
Sammy Beckett,
Sammy Someone,
Edna O'Brien,
Because she's a Woman,
And we're in enough trouble already,
Old Uncle Sammy Beckett and all,
And old Sammy Beckett and all.

(*Repeat verse to a dance.*)

CHAP: Well, now *I'm* going for a slash.

CHAIRMAN: And *I'm* going for a drink.

OLDER LADY: Is this the interval?

GIRL: The interval? You must be joking!

GRANDFATHER: Oh, can we go now?

CHAIRMAN: Everyone's free to do as they wish.

(*On the projection screen, there is a picture of the Trooping of the Colour. The men all stand up. Very brief, this.*)

(*To the audience.*) That wasn't actually meant to be disrespectful.

BOX MAN: Ha ha di-bloody ha ha! Where's the bar?

GIRL: By the men's loo, you drunken oaf.

INTERRUPTER: Take it off!

CAST: (*To the INTERRUPTER.*) You take yourself off.

(*They all turn and dance off to the tune of 'The Laughing Samba'. As the auditorium lights come up, the CHAIRMAN returns and starts to turn the handle of the barrel organ which plays 'Roll out the Barrel'. He then signals to the prompt corner. The STAGE MANAGER appears to take over the handle, the CHAIRMAN looks at his watch and saunters off. After a few moments, the STAGE MANGER, clearly bored by the barrel organ, stops turning it, and goes off as well.*)

End of Act One.

ACT TWO

As the audience returns, if indeed it does return, the house lights are up and an extremely loud Pop Group is blaring out over the loudspeakers, against the Pop Group's still photograph on the projection screen. On stage, the STAGE MANAGEMENT and STAGE HANDS and so on are dancing, some in an offhand and some in a rather demented manner. After a while, and the STAGE MANAGER will have to decide on this, when what is left of the house has got back in, some of them will look at their watches and start to wander off the stage.

The BOX MAN does his usual entrance, clutching a crate of brown ale, one bottle of which he is tippling. He smiles cheerily round at the audience, standing up and waving at them.

BOX MAN: This sounds a bit more like it! I came here to be *entertained*, I don't know about you.

INTERRUPTER: (*Settling into his seat.*) So did I. Doesn't seem very likely *now*. That Box Office Manager was quite insulting.

BOX MAN: Dead right, sonny boy! So he was to me. Right gaffer's man you've got in there. Boss's man. (*Shouting at the stage.*) Well, get on with it! (*Down to the INTERRUPTER.*)

I complained about the toilet.

INTERRUPTER: Good... I've got a tube to catch.

BOX MAN: Never you mind, sonny boy. If it doesn't buck up a bit, we'll all have a few jars and a general piss up. (*He smiles broadly around him.*) Okay? (*He starts to sing.*)
Why are we waiting,
Why are we waiting...

INTERRUPTER: (*Joining in.*) Why are we waiting,
Oh why, oh why...
(*The STAGE MANAGER appears.*)

STAGE MANAGER: That won't get you very far, you know.

BOX MAN: It won't get *you* any bloody far either, if you're not careful. Just get on with it. They burn down places like this, you know.

INTERRUPTER: Oh, I don't believe in violence. But I don't see why one should sit and be insulted. Quiet protest is quite sufficient.

STAGE MANAGER: All right. Start Dim.

(*He goes off, and the house lights do indeed start to dim as the FATHER enters and sits down at the piano. He starts playing and sings a snatch of 'On The Isle Of Capri'. He then sings 'In A Little Gypsy Tea-Room' as his son, the CHAP, enters. They sing together.*)

FATHER/CHAP: 'In a little gypsy tearoom,

    You stole my heart away,

    It was in a little gypsy tearoom,

    I fell in love one day…'

(*The GIRL enters.*)

GIRL: And he's such a thumping cad…

(*The CHAP sings to his FATHER's accompaniment, addressing himself to the GIRL.*)

CHAP: 'I am only a strolling vagabond,

    So good night, pretty maiden, good night,

    I am off to the hills and the valleys beyond,

    Good night…'

INTERRUPTER: Joan Littlewood did this years ago.

CHAP: 'Good night…'

GIRL: (*To the INTERRUPTER.*) Piss off.

BOX MAN: Yes, give the boy a chance.

CHAP: 'So good night, pretty maiden, good night.

    I come from the hills,

    And the valleys beyond,

    So good night, pretty maiden, good night.'

GIRL: All right. That'll do. (*To the BOX MAN.*) He's no boy.

BOX MAN: I want to see Val Doonican.

CHAP: And the Black and White Minstrels.

GIRL: Oh, he'll black up for you if you like.

INTERRUPTER: I like something entertaining, but that leaves you with something to think about afterwards.

GIRL: Well, forget it.

(*During this exchange, the CHAIRMAN enters and starts to sing, again to the FATHER's accompaniment.*)

CHAIRMAN:, 'Oh, my love is like a red, red rose...'
   (*To the audience.*) Join in all you old folks – we still need
   your money while you're here –
GIRL: Oh, my God! *His* love!
CHAIRMAN: 'That's newly sprung in June...'
   (*To the audience.*) And all you youngsters too, even if you
   can't remember the words. You'll be with us a bit longer
   if you're lucky.
BOX MAN: We don't want any of that modern rubbish.
GRANDFATHER: 'Everyone suddenly burst out singing...'
CHAIRMAN: 'Oh, my love is like the melody
   That's sweetly played in tune...'
   (*To the GIRL.*) I do hope you're not going to be cheap
   and obvious about the Scots.
GIRL: I couldn't he bothered, actually.
   (*She immediately dances to a number by the Supremes with
   the CHAP. This lasts as long as it will seem to hold.*)
   (*To the CHAP.*) You're not very good, are you?
CHAP: No...
   (*Once again, while this has been going on, the GRANDFATHER
   has entered and sat down on his chair. There is a silence, or
   if there isn't a silence, the actors will have to improvise.
   However, when the next stage is reached, the GRANDFATHER
   rises slowly and also sings.*)
GRANDFATHER: 'Rock of ages cleft for me,
   Let me hide myself in thee,' (*etc.*)
CHAP: Very good.
GIRL: Of course he's good.
INTERRUPTER: 'Ancient and Modern' now, is it?
BOX MAN: Sounds *bloody* ancient to me. Who wants a
   brown ale?
CHAIRMAN: (*To the BOX MAN.*) I shouldn't overplay it too
   much.
BOX MAN: Don't you get grotty with me! She's dead right.
   (*Pointing at the GIRL.*) You're just a moaning old posh-
   voiced pouf.
   (*The OLDER LADY enters.*)
   Come on, darling, sing us a song, or show us your knickers.

OLDER LADY: I will if you like.

CHAIRMAN: (*To the OLDER LADY.*) What *are* you going to do?

FATHER: *I* know.

(*He starts to sing as he plays the piano a fair pastiche of Jack Buchanan.*)

'Good night, Vienna,

You golden city of a thousand dreams...'

(*As he plays and sings, the OLDER LADY and the GRAND-FATHER execute a very dashing tango together. The BOX MAN applauds at the end of it.*)

INTERRUPTER: God, how sentimental!

BOX MAN: Give the old bag a break, or I'll come down and give you a right duffing up.

OLDER LADY: (*To the BOX MAN.*) Thank you very much.
(*The FATHER does his introduction to 'If You were The Only Girl In The World' and the OLDER LADY sings to the audience.*)

'If I were the only girl in the world,'

GRANDFATHER: (*Rising.*) 'And I was the only boy,'

CHAP: (*Also rising and singing.*) 'Nothing else would matter in the world today,'

GIRL: (*Rising and singing and taking the CHAP's hand.*)
'We would go on loving in the same old way.'

OLDER LADY/GRANDFATHER/CHAP/GIRL: (*All join hands and sing the rest of the chorus.*)

...'If you were the only girl in the world

And I was the only boy.'

INTERRUPTER: Oh God, I can't stand any more of this.

BOX MAN: Bloody good.

(*The CHAIRMAN lifts his eyes to heaven or at least somewhere above his usual line of vision and addresses the INTERRUPTER.*)

CHAIRMAN: I think I really do have to agree with you this time.

INTERRUPTER: And so you should. (*He gets up and goes out.*)

BOX MAN: Piss off!

GIRL: (*To the BOX MAN.*) Thank you, sir, she said.

BOX MAN: You know what *you* need.

GIRL: Yes, you told us all that before.

CHAIRMAN: Does anyone remember where we were?

GIRL: You must be mad.

(*The BOX MAN rises and sings.*)

BOX MAN: 'Oh, he's football crazy,

He's football mad,

Since he joined the local football club...'

CHAIRMAN: I know – 'He's lost the wee bit of sense he had.'

GIRL: If I were a man, my balls would hurt.

CHAP: Well, thank God you're not.

CHAIRMAN: Anyway, it's 'footba' crazy', not 'foot*ball*'. Anyone can see *you're* not a Scot.

BOXMAN: Show us your kilt! What's your tartan, then? The Macpouves I suppose.

CHAIRMAN: (*Wearily.*) I had an idea you were going to say that.

GIRL: We *all* had an idea he was going to say that.

CHAIRMAN: Yes, now this Chap was going to tell us about his life.

GIRL: That's what we're all afraid of.

CHAIRMAN: So, old um –

GIRL: Chap.

CHAIRMAN: I think the floor is what they call 'yours'.

BOXMAN: Give him a big hand! He's only just started. You never know. You might see him on the telly one day.

GIRL: Best place for him.

CHAIRMAN: Hear, hear.

(*The CHAP goes over to his FATHER at the piano and puts his arm round his shoulders.*)

CHAP: You needn't sit there all the time, you know.

FATHER: No, it's all right, I quite like sitting here.

GIRL: You've already said he's dead anyway.

GRANDFATHER: Missed the twentieth century. I didn't...

OLDER LADY: No, neither did I. I'm rather glad, aren't you?

CHAP: No.

BOX MAN: We shouldn't have missed *you*.
    (*The INTERRUPTER appears from another part of the house.*)
INTERRUPTER: Yes, I'd like to know what you'd have
    done without decent dentists and anaesthetics. Can't see
    you biting on to a leather belt.
CHAP: Nor you, either.
BOX MAN: Let him say his piece. It's a free country.
CHAIRMAN: It's not a free country.
BOX MAN: It's not a free country.
CHAP: As I was about to say –
    (*The GIRL goes into another Supremes type dance, the CHAP
    joins her. The music finishes suddenly.*)
CHAP: (*To the GIRL.*) Finished?
GIRL: Yes. Do carry on.
CHAP: As I was saying –
BOX MAN: What was he saying? This brown ale they sold
    me in the bar tastes like old horse piss.
GIRL: How would you know?
CHAP: ...I was born –
GIRL: That's a promising start.
CHAP: And original too.
CHAIRMAN: Oh, do stop it, the two of you. (*To the CHAP.*)
    Do you think you could get on with it?
INTERRUPTER: What do you mean 'get on with it'?
    He hasn't started yet.
BOX MAN: Give the boy a chance.
    (*The CHAP advances downstage and taking his time, he surveys
    the audience and addresses them. – If there are still any left.*)
CHAP: The last time that I saw the King,
    He did the most curious thing,
    With a nonchalant flick,
    He pulled out his dick,
    And said: 'If I *play*, will you *sing*?'
INTERRUPTER: Filth!
GIRL: Just bloody boring.
BOX MAN: I was in my cradle when I heard that one.
GIRL: Cradles weren't invented when *you* were born.
CHAP: I am going to make a sort of shortish speech about
    my life and women.

GIRL: Wouldn't you guess?

BOX MAN: Why, I've had more –

CHAP: Yes, than hot dinners. Except my dinners were probably a bit hotter and slightly more interesting.

BOX MAN: I'll come down and sort you out too!

CHAP: No, you won't.

CHAIRMAN: Yes, he's quite right. You're just an underpaid –

GIRL: Overworked –

CHAIRMAN: Exactly. What was it?

GIRL: 'Device' is what you keep saying.

CHAP: Now the first girl I really remember lusting after –

GIRL: Wake me up when he's finished.

CHAP: Was actually a woman.

(*They all change places and take up TV chat show poses.*)
I don't know what age she was really. She could have been twenty-one or thirty-one. All I remember is that she had a small boy called Malcolm about three years old, I should imagine, and a bit younger than me.

(*The CHAIRMAN clears his throat and becomes the interviewer to all the others.*)

CHAIRMAN: Now, J. Waddington Smith, you've just come from this play tonight – Did you think it came off at all? Or would you call it a total disaster?

GRANDFATHER: Not a total disaster, no. On the other hand –

GIRL: On the other hand –

GRANDFATHER: I must confess it did have *some* enjoyable moments.

CHAP: Oh, say that would you?

OLDER LADY: I quite enjoyed it. But then I suppose I'm easily pleased.

GIRL: Oh no, you're not. You're the worst audience in the world.

CHAP: Usual easy obligatory cracks about critics.

OLDER LADY: Well, naturally.

GIRL: (*Fiddling with her hair.*) But he really has got a bit too predictable now, hasn't he? (*To the CHAIRMAN.*) They are getting me fiddling with my hair in the intellectual winsome bit, aren't they?

CHAIRMAN: Yes, but I shouldn't worry about it too much. I've already told them that –

GIRL: Device –

CHAIRMAN: Up in the Box not to overdo it too much.

OLDER LADY: Quite right.

CHAIRMAN: (*To the CHAP.*) It struck me that there was a certain amount of strident waffle. What would you say to that?

CHAP: Oh, I agree. After all, there ought to be a bit more to it than that?

GIRL: Oughtn't there?

CHAIRMAN: I agree. Didn't there? What did you think about the devices?

CHAP: The theatrical ones, you mean?

GIRL: Well, we did go to the *theatre*, didn't we?

FATHER: What *is* all this?

CHAP: They call it television.

GIRL: Yes, you really died before all that.

CHAP: Lucky old bugger.

CHAIRMAN: We're having a 'lively intellectual confrontation'.

CHAP: 'Making the news'.

CHAIRMAN: Do you mind? 'The first with the news'. (*Rising.*) I think we've *done* this for the moment, anyway, don't you?

CHAP: Oh, yes.

(*They all change around seats with the CHAP now in the middle.*)

Oh, yes… The lady with the three year old boy.

GIRL: Malcolm.

INTERRUPTER: Why don't you give the young people a chance?

CHAP: Why don't you give us a chance?

BOX MAN: You take a chance, darling.

GIRL: Don't be disgusting.

CHAIRMAN: Why shouldn't he be? He's paid his money. As he says.

GIRL: I doubt it.

BOX MAN: And I want it back!

INTERRUPTER: So do I.

> (*All sing the Stoke City football song 'We'll Be With You',
> which also plays over the loud speakers, led by the BOX MAN,
> who twirls his scarf, etc., bawling, while some of the cast
> stand up to the Wembley type stadium sound.*)

CHAP: Well, to continue if that's possible –

CHAIRMAN: If anything's possible...

CHAP: There were the twins. One was called Gloria,
I know. And I think the other was Pat. But Pat was the
nice one, Gloria was the dirty one.

GIRL: Oh, yes.

CHAP: Then there was a younger, blonde fat one, but
I don't remember her name. But I do think she was more
sort of humiliating than the rest. Then there was my
Auntie Viv. She had very dark, curly hair.

FATHER: I used to call her the Gypsy Queen.

CHAP: That's right. But she had a funny way with handling
the children. And I remember she said to me, 'Don't lift
your trousers' – we used to wear what were called 'short
trousers' then – 'when you go to the toilet'.

GIRL: Are you going to go on much longer?

CHAP: Then there was Arabella.

GIRL: Arabella!

CHAP: Yes. She was twenty-one and I was about ten.

GIRL: And you 'would have died for her'.

CHAP: Yes, I would have died for her. She had a young
man, who was an old man of twenty-eight. And we all
three of us used to go for walks on the Downs. In the fog
with the destroyers wailing and the invisible convoys.

GIRL: How romantic.

CHAP: Not at all. He (*Pointing to the FATHER.*) was dying
of TB.

GRANDFATHER: Oh well, they used to die of it then.

CHAP: Like *flies*, in my family. My sister went and my
God, did I resent it. What she left *me* lumbered with.

GIRL: Next.

CHAP: Next? Oh yes. Then there was Betty. She was a
Brown Owl. And then a strapping great Girl Guide.

Christ, I was mad about *her*. I used to follow her down the streets from school – it was a state school I suppose you'd call it – and pretend I wasn't.

GIRL: What did she look like?

CHAP: Can't quite remember. But very dark blue eyes and hair – thick. Showed her legs off a lot but not too much.

GIRL: Very sensible. Next.

CHAP: There was somebody, I think she was called Audrey. She was a frightful bully and had a gang of boys mostly and used to sit on your head and try to suffocate you. Red hair, I think.

GIRL: Ginger minge in your nostrils. That must have been nice.

CHAP: Then there was Gladys.

GRANDFATHER: I used to know a Gladys.

GIRL: Who doesn't? What about her?

CHAP: Nothing much, really. She just said one day she'd only ever really liked me because I had wavy hair.

GIRL: How awful.

CHAP: I suppose it was fashionable at the time.

GIRL: Why does it have to *be about* anything?

CHAIRMAN: The Second World War…

GIRL: Vietnam…

CHAIRMAN: 'Luxuriantly bleak' I would say, wouldn't you?

CHAP: Yes, but 'martially lyrical'.

GIRL: Images! Who wants them? You can have them any old time.

OLDER LADY: I suppose it's all really just about things like music and fucking.

CHAIRMAN: Yes, but I suppose we've got to *discuss* it.

GIRL: (*To the CHAP.*) Yes?

CHAP: I don't think I can.

GIRL: Oh, don't start blubbing, it's too early.

CHAIRMAN: Much too early.

CHAP: I can't go through the *whole* list.

GIRL: We're not asking you to. Next.

CHAP: Then there was Shirley and her sister.

GIRL: What about them?

CHAP: I just wonder what happened to them, that's all.

GIRL: Well, we all wonder that sort of thing.

CHAP: Shut up, you lousy bitch. I wouldn't tell you anyway.

GIRL: And then?

CHAP: Well, believe it or not, there was Fanny.

BOX MAN: Annie and Fanny!

CHAP: That's right. The Fan Dancer who fell down on her Fan.

BOX MAN: Do you know the one about the crocodile shoes?

GIRL: Yes.

OLDER LADY: Oh yes, *I've* heard that one. It's awfully good.

BOX MAN: Are you bloody sure you've heard it?

CHAIRMAN: Yes.

BOX MAN: I'll bet you don't know what it's –

CHAP: Yes. It's got *three* punch lines.

CHAIRMAN: Next.

CHAP: Then there was Rosemary.

GIRL: (*To the INTERRUPTER.*) There's Rosemary for *you.*

INTERRUPTER: We don't know who any of these people *are.* What they're *doing.* Where it's taking *place.* Or anything!

OLDER LADY: Give the boy a chance.

CHAP: What? Oh, Rosemary.

GIRL: Yes, Rosemary.

CHAP: Ah yes, well, she had the rags up all the time.

GRANDFATHER: Well, they can't help it, you know.

CHAIRMAN: Well, he's got a point there.

CHAP: No, but she had it all the bloody time. I mean like all over the graveyard in Norwich Cathedral.

GIRL: Norwich – you mean like –

CHAIRMAN Yes. (*Wearily.*) Knickers off ready when I come home.

CHAP: I mean, Women's *Insides.* I've been walled up in them and their despairs and agony ever since I can remember.

GIRL: Perhaps you should try it yourself.

CHAP: I'm not strong enough.

GIRL: No, you're not.

INTERRUPTER: I think this sort of talk is highly
  embarrassing. My own wife is in the audience and I may
  say that she is undergoing, what I can only call to
  someone like you, an extremely difficult –

GIRL: Period –

INTERRUPTER: No. I would say more than that. Expected
  but dramatic experience in her life.

GIRL: You mean she's got the Hot Flushes?

CHAP: Well, let me tell you, mate, *I've* had them for
  forty years.

GIRL: And you look it... So we've got to Rosemary.

CHAIRMAN: Yes.

CHAP: Oh, I don't remember them. Then there was Jean,
  I suppose.

GIRL: (*Dances and sings.*) 'Jean, Jean...'

BOX MAN: You'll get no awards for *this* lot.

CHAP: She was really good and big and well-stacked and
  knew how to –

GIRL: Get you on the job.

CHAP: Christ, I was only nineteen! I could do it nine times
  in the morning.

CHAIRMAN: Nine times. Could you really?

GIRL: There's not much impressive in that.

CHAP: (*In a bad Scots accent.*) 'Oh, there's not much
  impressive in that'. We've all had *colds.*

GIRL: And then there are all those dreary wives of yours.

CHAP: That's right. Those dreary wives of mine... They all
  think I'm a pouf.

GIRL: I'm not surprised.

OLDER LADY: I don't think she should have said that
  to him.

GRANDFATHER: I don't know what they are talking
  about. *Any* of them.

CHAP: The first one was pretty good in the sack.

GIRL: So you keep telling us. She looks pretty awful *now.*

CHAP: My fault.

CHAIRMAN: I don't think I'm being compromising but –

GIRL: But –

43

CHAIRMAN: Well, I do feel, and I know you're going to yawn or laugh –

BOX MAN: Sing us a song!

CHAIRMAN: We will, my friend, I'm afraid we certainly will.

CHAP: Oh yes.

CHAIRMAN: But there are certain dark, painful places we shouldn't expose – for our own sakes and those of others.

CHAP: Actresses are pretty rotten lays.

GIRL: So are actors.

OLDER LADY: I've just been reading some material that's been sent to me.

GIRL: What's *she* on about?

OLDER LADY: They seem to call it pornographic. But it looks quite interesting to me.

GIRL: So it would, you dirty old bitch.

BOX MAN: I watch TV most nights of the week and all I can say is that the general standard of programmes is deplorable.

CHAP: Say that again.

BOX MAN: Deplorable.

CHAP: That's better.

OLDER LADY: (*Reading from brochure.*) 'This month we've got "The Virgin Bride was to be Raped".' How fascinating. 'This is the lead novelette. Then after "The Letters to Lucille" –'

GIRL: Who's Lucille?

OLDER LADY: I don't quite know. It doesn't say. But it goes on: 'We have a picture story about what a released convict is going to do to the first woman he sees when he gets out.'

BOX MAN: Come on, let's have a bit of *that*, then.

OLDER LADY: 'Next comes Part Two of "Sex in a Scout Camp". After that, Part Two of a novelette called "Young Orgy".'

BOX MAN: Get in there, it's your birthday.

CHAIRMAN: (*Despairingly.*) We really do have to get rid of him, don't we? I mean we *are* all *agreed*?

INTERRUPTER: Get rid of the lot of you, I say.

OLDER LADY: (*Reading.*) 'Then we finish with a girl masturbating herself in both her holes at one time.'

BOX MAN: Brown ale, anybody?

(*The lights dim and on the projection screen appears a column of marching British sailors. In the meantime, on the loudspeaker, the Band of the Royal Marines plays 'A Life on the Ocean Waves', naturally, at full blast. The BOX MAN joins in. When this has finished, the CHAIRMAN speaks, as do the others, and the same ritual is repeated more or less after each piece of so-called pornography is gravely but interestedly intoned by the OLDER LADY.*)

CHAIRMAN: 'Oh wad some Pow'r the gifte gie us,
To see oursels as others see us!
It wad frae mony a blunder free us,
And foolish notion.'

CHAP: 'Oh England, full of sin, but most of sloth;
Spit out thy phlegm, and fill thy breast with glory.'

GIRL: 'Love is a circle that doth restless move.'

CHAP: (*At GIRL.*) 'I do love, I know not what;
Sometimes this, and sometimes that.'

GRANDFATHER: 'Some days before death
When food's tasting sour on my tongue,
Cigarettes long abandoned,
Disgusting now even champagne;
When I'm sweating a lot
From the strain on a last bit of lung
And lust has gone out
Leaving only the things of the brain;
More worthless than ever
Will seem all the songs I have sung,
More harmless the prods of the prigs,
Remoter the pain,
More futile the Lord Civil Servant –'

CHAIRMAN: I think that perhaps at this stage we should say something else.

INTERRUPTER: You're telling us!

CHAIRMAN: Yes, well, you *may* have your chance later, my friend.

'I see phantoms of hatred and of the Heart's Fullness and
of the Coming Emptiness.'
(*The CHAIRMAN comes downstage and addresses everyone.*)
Yes, just wait a moment.
'I turn away and shut the door, and on the stair
Wonder how many times I could have proved my worth
In something that all others understand or share;
But oh! ambitious heart, had such a proof drawn forth
A company of friends, a conscience set at ease,
It had but made us pine the more. The abstract joy,
The half-read wisdom of demonic images,
Suffice the ageing man as once the growing boy.'
BOX MAN: We don't wish –
CHAIRMAN: No, my friend, and you may well be right.
　　But we are all plagiarists, as even you. As Brecht said
　　once and Shakespeare better than us all.
GIRL: He's getting quite good, isn't he?
OLDER LADY: (*Reading again.*) '"Waterloo Bridge". The
　　classic story as in the film of a young girl met and
　　seduced by an officer during the Blitz of London. She
　　gets fucked in a bomb shelter while sitting beside some
　　people that take no notice –'
CHAP: Take no notice?
GIRL: Well, I suppose it's sort of sophisticated.
OLDER LADY: 'Then when he leaves her, she meets a
　　lesbian who puts her on the street as a brass nail.'
GIRL: What's a brass nail?
CHAP: Don't ask me, I'm only here for the beer.
BOX MAN: Ha ha di-bloody ha ha! Taking the piss out of
　　us little people again.
　　(*On the projection screen an image of a shy and beautiful
　　Edwardian girl. From the loudspeakers the sweet draining sound
　　of the soprano in Handel's 'The Ode to Saint Cecilia's Day'.*)
　　'But oh, what art can teach,
　　What human voice can reach,
　　The sacred organ's praise.'
CHAIRMAN: 'Now we maun totter down, John,
　　And hand in hand we'll go,
　　And sleep thegither at the foot, John Anderson, my jo.'

GIRL: 'Men are suspicious; prone to discontent;...'

CHAIRMAN: 'Subjects still loathe the present Government.'

GRANDFATHER: 'This is the time of day when the weight
of bedclothes

Is harder to bear than a sharp incision of steel.

The endless anonymous croak of a cheap transistor

Intensifies the lonely terror I feel.'

(*The CHAP goes over to his FATHER at the piano.*)

CHAP: (*Gently.*) Come and sit down. It's all over for you.

GRANDFATHER: Well, it was all over for him thirty
years ago.

FATHER: (*Allowing himself to be led to a chair.*) I am as old as
the century.

GIRL: So you say.

OLDER LADY: (*Reading.*) 'Number fifty-three. Did you ever
fancy getting hold of a pretty young girl-scout and
fucking her up the arsehole? Well, the two lucky lads in
this picture story did just that. You see this lovely young
girl was canvassing through their apartment block while
they were in the process of screwing this girl, from both
front and back. Well, when the girl-scout rang their bell
they got the girl to get dressed and coax her in; once
they got her inside they stripped her and gave her such a
fucking she'll never forget it. Both of them get up her
tiny little arsehole. GREAT.'

(*On the projection screen, a scene from the final ensemble of
'Der Rosenkavalier', the sweeping melody for the Marschallin,
and so on.*)

'*Hab mirs gelobt, ihn lieb – zu haben.*'

CHAIRMAN: 'She is a winsome wee thing,

She is a handsome wee thing,

She is a lo'esome wee thing.

This sweet wee wife of mine.'

BOX MAN: Nancy Gobble Job, you mean!

GIRL: (*To CHAP.*) 'Give me a kiss, and to that kiss a score;

Then to that twenty, add a hundred more:

A thousand to that hundred: so kiss on,

To make that thousand up a million.

Treble that million, and when that is done,
Let's kiss afresh, as when we first begun.'
CHAP: Oh, shut up, you silly bitch.
OLDER LADY: (*Reading.*) 'A picture story of hard rape! Six
men drinking in a small bar in Germany decide to grab
the pretty little blonde barmaid and have a giggle with
her but, as many things do, it went wrong. She resisted!
They ganged up on her and tore her clothes off of her
and proceeded to violate her in every way that they
could. Each one had a go at fucking her, some in her
bum, some in her mouth. They held her on the table and
screwed until she finally passed out from the spunk
forced down her throat. I have seen some rape scenes
while I have been in this business, but *WOW*.'
CHAIRMAN: 'Tho' poor in gear, we're rich in love.'
CHAP: 'Bid me to live, and I will live
Thy Protestant to be:…'
BOX MAN: Watch it, you've got some of your bleeding
Catholics out here!
CHAIRMAN: Just ignore him.
CHAP: 'Or bid me love, and I will give
A loving heart to thee.
A heart as soft, a heart as kind,
A heart as sound and free
As in the whole world thou canst find,
That heart I'll give to thee.'
GIRL: 'My true love hath my heart and I have his,
By just exchange one for the other giv'n;
I hold his dear, and mine he cannot miss,
There never was a better bargain driv'n.'
GRANDFATHER: '"O words are lightly spoken"
Said Pearse to Connolly,
"Maybe a breath of politic words
Has withered our Rose Tree;
Or maybe but a wind that blows
Across the bitter sea."'
OLDER LADY: 'Homo Action Number Five. As the cover
picture shows we have found a young man who is double

jointed enough to suck his own cock whilst he is being fucked by a big prick.'

(*On the projection screen a large rose.*)

CHAIRMAN: I suppose they'll play something from 'Cosi fan tutte' now.

(*Naturally, the loudspeakers do.*)

GIRL: Of course.

CHAIRMAN: Well, I'll say this bit about the Rose anyway, and get it over with.

(*Fade music.*)

'And my fause lover stole my rose

But ah! he left the thorn wi' me.'

CHAP: Or, as he'd have said himself:

'Don't let the awkward squad fire over me.'

GRANDFATHER: I suppose it's all right. It seems a bit sad.

CHAP: Well, at least you can't frighten the horses

any longer.

OLDER LADY: (*Reading.*) 'Free offer. Two young teenage Sea Scouts are in the apartment of randy man; they were collecting for charity but they collected more than they bargained for. It didn't take him long to get their panties down and his big prick into their young mouths and cunts. Second Number Three. An efficiency expert comes into a humdrum office to get it running smoothly, then he gets the old maidenly bookkeeper in and shows her how to fuck, when he gets them all at it he leaves. VERY FUNNY AND GOOD!'

(*The FATHER begins to play and GRANDFATHER stands up and sings.*)

GRANDFATHER: 'Life like an ever-rolling stream

Bears all its sons away.

They fly forgotten as a dream...'

(*All join in including BOX MAN.*)

ALL: 'Dies at the opening day.'

BOX MAN: (*Applauding himself as much as anybody.*) That's a good one, that is.

INTERRUPTER: It's still filth and it always was.

49

(*Note: During the singing of the Hymn by the GRANDFATHER the projection screen shows an enormous ascending jet plane with the words 'If you want to get away, jet away'.*)

OLDER LADY: '"Panther Kidnap." Two young members of the Black Panthers kidnap a white girl on the street and take her back to their pad. There they tear her clothes from her and make her perform all sorts of sexual perversions. She tries to fight them off but these two blacks are much too powerful for her. Lots of good action.'

(*The FATHER does another Jack Buchanan and sings a few bars of 'Two Little Bluebirds'.*)

GIRL: 'I dare not ask a kiss;
I dare not beg a smile;
Lest having that, or this,
I might grow proud the while.

No, no, the utmost share,
Of my desire shall he
Only to kiss that air,
That lately kissed thee.'

CHAIRMAN: 'Doubt you to whom my Muse these notes
intendeth,
Which now to my breast o'ercharged to music lendeth?
To you, to you, all song of praises due;
Only in you my song begins and endeth.'

GIRL: 'Thy fair heart my heart enchained.'

CHAP: '"Fool!" Said my Muse, to me, "Look in thy heart and write."'

(*The stage lights dim a little while the loudspeakers play a few bars from 'The Lark Ascending'.*

As the music ends abruptly, so do the lights come up and the OLDER LADY continues with her next recitative.)

OLDER LADY: (*Reading.*) '"Dog Scene." Not wishing to get into trouble with you animal lovers let me state right here, that although this is a very good action film with two girls a man and a dog it is by no means all action with the dog. He does, however, do a very good job of fucking both the girls then the man takes over for the screwing while the dog watches. A GOODY!'

(*On the projection screen a long view of a densely trafficked motorway. On the loudspeakers a few bars of 'Dorabella' from the 'Enigma Variations'.*

Once again the music stops in almost mid bar as the lights snap on.)

GRANDFATHER: 'A man on his own in the car,
    Is revenging himself on his wife;
    He opens the throttle and bubbles with dottle
    And puffs at his pitiful life.

    "She's losing her looks very fast,
    She loses her temper all day;
    That lorry won't let me get past,
    This Mini is blocking my way.

    Why can't you step on it and shift her!
    I can't go on crawling like this!
    At breakfast she said that she wished I was dead –
    Thank heavens we don't have to kiss.

    I'd like a nice blonde on my knee
    And one who won't argue or nag.
    Who dares to come hooting at me?
    I only give way to a Jag."'

CHAP: 'Take thou of me smooth pillows, sweetest bed;
    A chamber deaf to noise and blind to light,
    A rosy garland and a weary head.'

OLDER LADY: '"Anal Fuck." If you have ever had a snooty girl working for YOU, perhaps you have felt like doing to her what these two bosses did to this girl; after she had destroyed several hours's hard work, they grabbed her and tore her clothes off and while one fucked her in her cunt the other stuck his prick up her arse. A very good film with excellent colour work.'

(*During the OLDER LADY's gentle declamation appears a fairly pretty contemporary young girl on the projection screen. Immediately this is finished, the loudspeakers play a few bars of 'The Nimrod variation' of Elgar. Stop.*)

CHAP: 'Her pretty feet
  Like snails did creep
  A little out, and then,
  As if they started at Bo-Peep,
  Did soon draw in agen.'
CHAIRMAN: 'Bid me to weep, and I will weep,
  While I have eyes to see.
  Bid me despair, and I'll despair,
  Under that cypress tree;
  Or hid me die, and I will dare
  E'en Death, to die for thee.'
CHAP: 'Thou art my life, my love, my heart,
  The very eyes of me:
  And hast command of every part,
  To live and die for thee.'
OLDER LADY: (*Reading.*) '"The Diver." Skin-diving
  enthusiasts will like this approach. Two girls bathing
  on a lonely beach suddenly find that they are being
  observed from beneath by a diver with an aqualung.
  He takes off one of the girls' bras and chases her up the
  beach for her pants; the other girl tries to help but she is
  soon stripped as well. Then lots of fucking. GREAT.'
  (*During this sequence, skin-divers, male and female, appear
  on the projection screen.*)
BOX MAN: I know where I'm going for my holidays next
  year.
CHAIRMAN: 'That sweet enemy, France.'
CHAP: 'They love indeed who quake to say they love.
  Oh heav'nly fool, thy most kiss-worthy face
  Anger invests with such lovely grace,
  That Anger's self I needs must kiss again.'
OLDER LADY: (*Reading.*) This one's called 'Straight Wife
  Swap'.
  (*On projection screen lone piper in kilt, possibly Ghurka.
  Plays 'The Flowers of the Forest'.*)
INTERRUPTER: (*As lights snap back on.*) What's all this
  thing about the Scots?
CHAIRMAN: 'No! The lough and the mountain, the ruins
                                              and rain

And purple blue distances bound your demesne,
For the tunes to the elegant measures you trod
Have chords of deep longing for Ireland and God.'

INTERRUPTER: Is this *ever* going to end?

BOX MAN: Sing us another song!

(*The stage lights darken and on the projection screen a picture of miners emerging from the pit appears. On the loudspeakers is played 'Cwm Rhondda'.*
The entire cast on stage stands with the exception of the GIRL. However, the BOX MAN stands up as reverently as he can with a bottle of beer to his lips.)

INTERRUPTER: Oh, it's the Welsh now, is it?

GIRL: (*To BOX MAN.*) What are you standing up for? You're not even Welsh.

BOX MAN: No, but they're the best rugby players we've got.

CHAIRMAN: Have you ever watched rugby?

BOX MAN: No, have you?

CHAIRMAN: No, but I went to Rugby school.

GIRL: You would.

BOX MAN: Up Chelsea!

OLDER LADY: (*Reading.*) 'A very good yarn about straight sex, lesbianism, feminine domination and flagellation.'
(*On screen, a picture of a young couple kissing one another, somewhat chastely, but with undoubted passion. During this, the FATHER plays on the piano and sings.*)

FATHER: 'I like a nice cup of tea in the morning
And a nice cup of tea with my tea,
And at half past eleven
My idea of heaven is a nice cup of tea.'

CHAIRMAN: (*Singing.*) 'And when it's time for bed,
There's a lot to be said
For a nice cup of tea!'

BOX MAN: 'For a nice cup of tea!'
(*He downs some more brown ale.*)

CHAP: 'Leave me, O love, which reacheth but to dust;
And thou, my mind, aspire to higher things;
Grown rich in that which never taketh rust;
Whatever fades, but fading pleasure brings.'

GRANDFATHER: 'Never love was so abused.'

(*To himself.*) I seem to remember that somewhere...

GIRL: (*To CHAP.*) 'O fair! O sweet! When I do look on thee,
In whom all joys so well agree,...'

CHAP: Lying bitch!

GIRL: Yes!

'Heart and soul do sing in me,
Just accord all music makes.'

OLDER LADY: (*Reading.*) '"The Rustlers"'! This one
appears to be, what does it say, oh yes, 'lesbian and
straight, this story is about cowboys'.

(*On the screen a picture of blind and gassed British soldiers
from the First World War. The music is 'The British
Grenadiers'. After the usual harsh snap-out the
GRANDFATHER rises again and talks almost to himself.*)

GRANDFATHER: It was seven-thirty a.m. on July the
First, 1916. That's when we went over the top.

INTERRUPTER: Yes, we know all that, 'sixty thousand
casualties and two for every yard of the front'.

CHAP: Not bad for all that.

GRANDFATHER: More like the end, if you like to say so.

CHAP: Obvious.

CHAIRMAN: True, nonetheless.

BOX MAN: We don't want to hear all about that.

CHAIRMAN: I think that's pretty clear.

FATHER: (*Sings.*) 'I'm on a seesaw;' 'Room five-o-four,'

OLDER LADY: (*Reads again.*) '"Slave Girl." Two stories of
whipping, spanking and sex.'

GIRL: 'Won't you change partners and dance...'

(*They all sit and listen rather dejectedly to 'Variations on a
Theme of Thomas Tallis', at some time during which the BOX
MAN, in a fit of generosity, starts to throw down bottles of
brown ale to the CHAIRMAN, who distributes them among
the actors and actresses.*)

BOX MAN: Here, have a drink on me.

(*To the audience*) Well, what are you all doing? Just fuck
all. I think they *need* a drink.

INTERRUPTER: *We* need something.

GIRL: We all do.

CHAP: I do... If I don't get it soon, I'll go potty.

GRANDFATHER: (*To BOX MAN.*) Your very good health, sir.

(*All the actors on the stage rise and toast the BOX MAN.*)

BOX MAN: Jolly good luck. What about a bit more of that stuff?

CHAP: (*Sings.*) 'They're writing songs of love,
But not for me.'

GIRL: (*Sings.*) 'Every time we say goodbye,
I die a little...'

OLDER LADY: Yes, of course. Where are my glasses?

BOX MAN: Someone kindly give this old lady her glasses.
(*The CHAP does so.*)

OLDER LADY: (*Reads.*) 'In time with the heaving of her own hips, Miss Twitch moderately beat the youth's bottom. The movement of her body increased –'

GIRL: Well, it would –

OLDER LADY: '– increased in its intensity with the strapping until she stiffened and sighed.' I think this one's rather dull. It just says 'Two Stories of whipping, spanking and sex.'

BOX MAN: Nothing wrong with that. Takes all sorts, you know.

CHAIRMAN: (*Leaning over to OLDER LADY.*) May I have a quick butchers?

OLDER LADY: Of course. My eyes are getting tired anyway.

GIRL: I was just hoping he wouldn't use rhyming slang. It's so fatiguing to listen to.

(*CHAIRMAN reads from the piece of paper.*)

CHAIRMAN: (*Reading.*) '"To Each His Own. He paused, waiting, and – sure enough, as with his finger Robin's bottom accepted this new degree of dilation; and the lad relaxed – so that he could thrust again – and force half the length... Another gasp and a temporary tensing resulted from this thrust – but this sudden clenching of Robin's rectum only added to the thrills that David was getting from the opening of this virginal bottom."

HOMOSEXUAL WITH A TINY BIT OF 'BI'.'

INTERRUPTER: Some of us, you know, did go out at the time and try and do something about all that and it did get done, like it or not.

BOX MAN: Quite right.

CHAP: Some of your best friends are pouves.

INTERRUPTER: And it ill behoves –

GIRL: I do like 'it ill behoves'.

CHAP: Not bad.

GIRL: (*To INTERRUPTER.*) Shut up, revue artist.

CHAP: Bullshit artist.

   'Too long a sacrifice
   Can make a stone of the heart.
   O when may it suffice?
   That is Heaven's part, our part
   To murmur name upon name –'

GRANDFATHER: 'They must to keep their certainty accuse
   All that are different of a base intent;
   Pull down established honour; hawk for news
   Whatever their loose fantasy invent
   And murmured with bated breath, as though
   The abounding gutter had been Helicon
   Or calumny a song. How can they know
   Truth flourishes where the student's lamp has shone,
   And there alone, that have no solitude?
   So the crowd come they care not what may come.
   They have loud music, hope every day renewed
   And heartier loves; that lamp is from the tomb.'

CHAIRMAN: I think we're mostly agreed about that.

INTERRUPTER: We most certainly are not.

BOX MAN: Give him another drink.

   (*He throws down another bottle of beer to the CHAIRMAN who does his best to catch it skilfully.*)

CHAIRMAN: Thank you.

   (*As he drinks from the bottle, the Union Jack appears on the screen and the loudest, most rousing version is heard of Blake's 'Jerusalem'.*)

INTERRUPTER: Oh God!

   (*He groans and moves off to the bar. The music snaps off again and the CHAIRMAN addresses the audience.*)

CHAIRMAN: Well, it's a sort of agreement.
  'No, no, not night but death;
  Was it needless death after all?'
CHAP: Cheers.
BOX MAN: God bless you. Is that *poetry*? Or just *talking*?
CHAIRMAN: Just talking.
  'For England may keep faith
  For all that is done and said.'
BOX MAN: Don't you worry. I *said* it was the World Cup
  this time. And I'll take on anybody!
CHAIRMAN: 'We know their dream; enough
  To know they dreamed and are dead;
  And what if excess of love
  Bewildered them till they died?'
CHAP: Just a minute before you sit down.
  (*He hails the STAGE MANAGER and he and the
  CHAIRMAN help to wheel on a pulpit. As they do so, the
  panatrope plays the Prisoners' song 'Durch Nacht Zum Licht'
  from 'Fidelio'. As soon as the pulpit is in place, the music
  stops, the STAGE MANAGER goes off and the CHAP
  addresses the GIRL.*)
CHAP: You, I think.
GIRL: Oh no, you. I can't do imitations.
CHAP: Well, you can, actually. Impressions, really. Which
  are much better. However. –
  (*He ascends the pulpit and addresses the theatre in a thick
  Belfast accent. As he does so, the projection screen shows a
  group of extremely tough-looking British troops in flak kit
  and riot masks etc, facing a crowd of Irish civilians. LC.*)
  And I say to you, the British people, and by that I mean
  the people of Northern Ireland, that not only myself but
  all decent proper-thinking people throughout the world,
  whether Protestant or Catholic, are shocked daily and
  troubled by the tragic sight of our troops who must be
  the best, as well as the most disciplined in the world,
  being incited physically, to say nothing of them morally
  and spiritually, of seeing them, having to stand inactive
  behind their shields while a lot of ignorant thugs and
  hooligans are pelting at them with their bombs and guns!

INTERRUPTER: There should be an Independent Inquiry.

BOX MAN: Quite right. Bloody hooligans.

GIRL: (*Turning on audience.*) Murdering British soldiers, they're all bloody murderers! You're all bloody murderers.

BOX MAN: Why don't you get back to Ireland and let us unemployed British get on with the job!?

GIRL: Who needs England?

BOX MAN: *You* do for a start.

CHAP: (*Descending from the pulpit.*) Right. Someone else carry on. I was running out of steam anyway.

GIRL: That was clear.

(*The CHAP assists the GIRL into the pulpit. During this, the Irish tricolour waves on the screen to an appropriate Gallic tune. The GIRL addresses the audience from the pulpit.*)

You all know what I think –

BOX MAN: I should say we do, we've heard it enough times.

GIRL: Well, it needs repeating to get into concrete skulls like yours. Get out of Ireland!

BOX MAN: Get out of England!

GIRL: Don't think I won't!

BOX MAN: Good!

GIRL: You've oppressed us for three centuries.

BOX MAN: What about it? Bloody idle lot. Think you're all poets and dreamers, I know. Shall I tell you something, mate? The only thing that ever came out of Ireland –

GIRL: I know, is horses and writers.

BOX MAN: And who said that?

GIRL: A lot of Horse Protestants. And I'll bet you didn't know who said that.

BOX MAN: Some bloody Catholic IRA man.

GIRL: You're damn right.

BOX MAN: Well, I bet he did a damn sight better in London than in Dublin.

GIRL: You're right –

BOX MAN: Do you want a brown ale? Of course I suppose you only drink bleeding Guinness.

GIRL: Stick your brown ale.

BOX MAN: And you stick your Guinness, and I hope –

GIRL: 'The ship goes down in Galway Bay.' That's the way with the lot of you.

CHAIRMAN: Oh dear, would anyone else like to say something?

INTERRUPTER: Yes.

BOX MAN: Shut your gob.

CHAIRMAN: Well, we do at least know that that's an Irish expression.

INTERRUPTER: I think it's all very well –

BOX MAN: Taking the piss out of the Irish –

INTERRUPTER: If you like. But what I object to, and I don't just say this on behalf of my wife –

GIRL: (*Descending from pulpit.*) You wouldn't.

INTERRUPTER: But, as I was going to say before you interrupted me, all these jibes about bigotry are all very well but personally I find the implicit condescension inherent –

CHAP: Inherent!

INTERRUPTER: Yes, sir, inherent. It's a perfectly proper word and expresses what I mean to say.

CHAP: Which is – ?

INTERRUPTER: That using a woman –

CHAP: As an object? Or were you going to say stereotype?

INTERRUPTER: Simply that you are being snide and coarse at the expense of a great many highly able and misused Women. Fortunately, you will no longer be able to get away with it.

CHAP: I didn't think I *had* got away with it. Perhaps I didn't try hard enough.

OLDER LADY: I quite agree with that gentleman. He is rather bad-mannered and silly, but, in this case, I think he's quite right. (*To the CHAIRMAN.*) May I say a few words?

CHAIRMAN: By all means do. You'll probably say something sensible.

OLDER LADY: Thank you. (*She has already ascended the pulpit.*) May I say first that I have no particular personal complaint. In some ways, I was born into a good time. And because of my natural intelligence, have managed to cope with what to most *men* would be an intolerable situation. My young friend here has complained, if I heard him correctly, of one of his earlier girlfriends being sick in the grounds of Norwich Cathedral. However, I would just say to him and others like him that it is a mere fact of life that women at all times and at all ages have suffered from, and in many cases died from, not merely childbirth but from what you would no doubt call the inbuilt tedium of organs such as the cervix, the vulvae, the vagina and the womb.

BOX MAN: Disgusting.

OLDER LADY: If men had to undergo what they so cheerfully call 'the curse' –

BOX MAN: Period pains –

OLDER LADY: – They would have long ago invented some alleviation.

BOX MAN: Invent it yourself. Sing us a song.

OLDER LADY: I'm afraid our young friend here has let him delude himself into dreaming about something he thinks of as 'Eternal Woman'.

BOX MAN: Who doesn't?

OLDER LADY: That is because she is only valued by the excitement she may or may not arouse.

BOX MAN: Get off out of it, you old bag.

OLDER LADY: In short, she has to be desirable.

BOX MAN: Well, it does help, lady.

OLDER LADY: In the case of men, it appears not to be necessary. We women can be put down, if that is the expression, by the flimsiest physical or intellectual failing. We have been eternally abandoned from the Old Testament onwards. All I say to you now is that we may all probably totally abandon you. Men, I mean.
(*She turns to the CHAP, who applauds.*)
Would you mind?

CHAP: Certainly.

(*He assists her down the steps although she seems to be in no real need of it.*)

My turn.

CHAIRMAN: Hurry it up a bit.

CHAP: Right ho, squire.

The nude is female by definition. Nudity is evasive, fleeing from description, allusive...

(*During this speech, various classic female nudes appear on the screen.*)

The naked male may be powerful, even beautiful, but self-defining like a jet aircraft in flight. Seldom is it more than technology made Flesh. Female, in this sense, is Art. The Male is Critic. Or, so it seems to me at this moment. Female is Art, secretive even when it conceals nothing. Revealing all, it is no sphinx for nothing, it contains and sustains life itself, taming random seed and even time. Making mystery of woman, the liberationists would say, is to belittle her in a glib religious conspiracy of fake mystery. Imprison her with the useful poetry of femininity and you destroy her in a cloud of voracious male imagination and inevitable social enslavement. The course of history! Woman is dead! Long live Woman!... I do not believe it. She has always triumphed in my small corner of spirit, just as I have failed *her* image – my broken, misty, self-deceiving image you may say – during most of my life. And, remembering it, what a long time it has been. I believe in Woman, whatever that may be, just as I believe in God, because they were both invented by man. If I am their inventor, they are my creators, and they will continue to exist. During most of my life. What made me think of it? Watching a couple in a street late at night in a provincial town. Being in love, how many times and over such a period. Being in Love! What anathema to the Sexual Militant, the wicked interest on free capital. Anathema because it involves waste, exploitation of resources, sacrifice, unplanned expenditure, both sides sitting down together in unequal desolation. *This* is the market place I have known and

wandered in almost as long as I indecently remember or
came to forget. Being in love, quaint expense of spirit,
long overripe for the bulldozer; of negotiating from the
strength of unmanning women's liberation. Those long-
shore bullies with bale hooks in bras and trousers
seamed with slogans and demands… Being in love.
Desolation in the sea of hope itself Sentimental? False?
Infantile? Possibly. And infantile because my memories
of the phenomenon, if there be such a one, is or ever will
be, start so *young*. From three, yes, I know it was three,
even till the only twenty-one, there were so many girls,
girl-women, women of all ages, I loved. Very few of
them were in love with me, alas. Being in love blunders
all negotiations and certainly differentials. I have been
sometimes indecently moved to tears and if there were a
court of justice in these things, I would have been dealt
with summarily as a persistent offender, asking for
innumerable, nameless and unspeakable offences to be
taken into account. However, if I have been such a
villain in this manor of feelings, I have tried to be as
clever as I know how. Knowing, as we all know, that
there is no such thing. If I have used blunt instruments
and sophisticated gear, I've tried to avoid soft risks and
only go for the big stuff. Naturally, I've made mistakes.
In fact, when you look at it, the successful jobs have been
far fewer than the fair cops. But that is the nature of
crime itself, of *being in love*, you are incapable of adding
up the obvious odds against you, unlike the law-abider
with his common sense and ability to discriminate
between his own needs and that of the rest of society. To
sustain and endure beneath the law –

GIRL: *Beneath*, naturally –

CHAP: – Being in love is a crime against women, and
yes, oh yes, reducing them to objects – as this splendid
lady has pointed out. To fantasies of poetry, poetry
and piety and bourgeois poetry, notwithstanding the
workers at that. It demeans men and serves their
historic despotism, whatever you think, over the

female. So much is said; so let it be so. It has not been the truth to *my* past; though it may well be that of one who has been a truly conniving peasant toiling under vicious and unnerving tyranny. The revolution is about to break, comrades, and I for one shall not wait to be explainable or forced heads down in the opening wave of forced collective. *Girls past.* If I ever yearned for a figment England, so I yearned for *them*; for girls past, fewer in the present and sadly, probably in the future. Who *were* they? All I remember most is their names, what they wore, sometimes what they looked like. Not very much.

GIRL: You've said that about four hundred times.

CHAP: So I have. Yes. I have indeed...

(*He descends from the pulpit and he and the GIRL clasp each other.*)

GIRL: Heart of my heart...

CHAP: Heart of *my* heart...

GIRL: People don't fall in love. (*To audience.*) *That* idea is no longer effective in the context of modern techniques. We are not nations or nation states. All that must go. We are part of an efficient, maximum productive ECONOMIC UNION. And Economic Unions do not fall in love. They amalgamate. They cut down. They are Now in the Land's future. We are that Land and we are on the brink of Progress. Even Progress has its cliché programmer. But there. We have nothing but gain to contemplate. Loss, such as it may have been, is, has been, ground into the shining, kindly present even that is *ours* already! Even at this moment. We are tearing down. We build! We build *now*. And NOW. We are not language. We are lingua. We do not love, eat or cherish. We *exchange.* Oh yes: we talk. We have words, rather: environment; pollution; problems; *issues*; oh, and – So century, century as is and will be – *APPROCHE MOI. Approche moi.* To me...

(*The GIRL turns from the audience and kisses the CHAP.*)

CHAP: Oh, heart, dearest heart. What does *that* mean! Rhetoric. I do, I have, I've wanted you, want you, will,

may not and so on. I love you, yes. I shall. Shan't.
Heart... And I want, yes – here we go – want to fuck
you... Not cum-uppance or any of that... Heart: I want
you. Legs high. High. Open. Prone: if you like. We can
both laugh. And enjoy. Enjoy me if you can. I *do* enjoy
you. I *do.* I want you, thighs enveloping my head. Mist.
I shall want to breathe... Give me *you.* I'll do what I can
with me. I hate to use the words between us – but –
I want what I know, have known, we know has taken,
done, enjoyed, laughed over; cherished. Between us. Girl.
Chap. We are lost without... You *know.* Don't you?

GIRL: Yes. I really think – perhaps – I do.

CHAP: Do. Don't. Will. Won't. Can. Can't. I wish I were
inside you. Now. At this moment... However.

GIRL: So do I. *However...*

BOX MAN: Very nicely expressed.

CHAIRMAN: What do you know about it?

BOX MAN: If I may be allowed to say so.

(*Everyone in the cast looks up at the BOX MAN, with the
exception of the GIRL and the CHAP who are intent upon
each other.*)

CAST: Piss off.

CHAIRMAN: (*Sings to the FATHER's accompaniment.*)
My balls are like a red, red rose.

BOX MAN: What time is it, for Christ's sake?

GIRL: (*To the CHAP.*) I've watched for you all my life.

CHAP: Likewise.

GIRL: And looked and wanted and as you would say,
observed.

(*BOX MAN stands up and sings the opening bars of a patriotic
song. The auditorium is then almost bludgeoned by a recording
of the same song. After a few bars of this, the CHAIRMAN
gets up, holding his bentwood chair.*)

CHAIRMAN: Well, I think that'll have to do this time.

CHAP: It will.

CHAIRMAN: I'm not a good chairman at all.

INTERRUPTER: No!

CHAIRMAN: Very well, then –

(*He extends his hands to the rest of the cast and they all stand
hand in hand together and sing 'Widdecombe Fair' in its*)

original. During the song they produce bunting with the words on each piece THE – VERY – BEST – OF – BRITISH – LUCK.)

CAST: 'Tom Pearce, Tom Pearce,
Come lend me your grey mare,
All along, down along, out along lea,
For I want to go to Widdecombe Fair
With Peter Davey,
Dan'l Widden…'
(*And so on. CHAIRMAN addresses the audience.*)

CHAIRMAN: So: that's what you'd call your lot. *Our* lot…
And may the Good Lord bless you and keep you. Or
God rot you.
(*All the CAST hum 'When You Are Weary, Friend of Mine'
as they pick up their chairs and go off, leaving the
GRANDFATHER, who strums and sings 'Old Father
Thames'. He then goes off with his chair and the stage lights
dim as one of the stage management comes on and idly turns
the handle of the barrel organ.*
*The cast return to face the audience but with no sense of
'Taking A Call'. The INTERRUPTER boos and walks out,
the BOX MAN applauds enthusiastically and drinks some
more beer. The actors go off as the curtain falls.*)

The End.

Characters

LADY REGINE FRIMLEY

STAN ('MR' FRIMLEY)

WAIN

STELLA SHRIFT

LETITIA PANGBORN

MRS ISOBEL SANDS

LADY GWEN MITCHELSON

JOG FIENBERG

RACHEL, THE COUNTESS OF BLEAK

LEONARD GRIMTHORPE

SMASH DEEL

FREDERICK BLACK

STRATFORD WEST

JOHN STEWKES, M.P.

ASHLEY WITHERS

ROBERT BIGLEY

The End of me Old Cigar was first performed at the Greenwich Theatre, London, on 16 January 1975, with the following cast:

LADY REGINE FRIMLEY, Rachel Roberts

STAN ('MR' FRIMLEY), Neil Johnston

WAIN, Toby Salaman

STELLA SHRIFT, Sheila Ballantine

LETITIA PANGBORN, Angela Galbraith

MRS ISOBEL SANDS, Jill Bennett

LADY GWEN MITCHELSON, Jasmina Hilton

JOG FIENBERG, Marty Cruickshank

RACHEL, THE COUNTESS OF BLEAK, Joanna Lumley

LEONARD GRIMTHORPE, Keith Barron

SMASH DEEL, Roderic Leigh

FREDERICK BLACK, Ian Milton

STRATFORD WEST, Kenneth Macgarvie

JOHN STEWKES MP, Charles Kinross

ASHLEY WITHERS, John Grillo

ROBERT BIGLEY, Mike Lucas

Director, Max Stafford Clark

ACT ONE

Scene: *Frimley House.*

The sitting-room of large country house. It should be very large. Jacobean, perhaps, with Knole sofas. Anyway, whatever period, furnished in the most circumspect taste and careful-careless luxury, reflecting a little on the extravagant nature of its owner, LADY REGINE FRIMLEY. There are huge, elaborate mirrors everywhere. She is lying back, listening to the final trio of 'Der Rosenkavalier'. As she listens, enraptured, her 'husband' STAN, (she is a widow) sits reading the Melody Maker and various racing papers. She is about late thirties, slightly older than he. She is a most attractive woman, finely but comfortably dressed. He is rather the sort of man who poses in the nude for magazines or manages pop groups or boutiques. Presently, but not for a while, she brings the trio to an end by turning off the record player. Pause.

STAN: What you turn it off for? Any tips for the Gold Cup?

REGINE: Lady Be Good.

STAN: Get on. What's his form? Can't even find it here.
     Oh, yes… If the going's wet.

REGINE: One of the stewards told me. He put a hundred
     pounds on for me – to win, of course. And I've had a tip
     from the weather bureau…
     '*Es send die mehreren Dinge auf der Welt,*
     so dass sie ein's nicht glauben tät,
     wenn man sie möcht erzählen hor'n.
     Alleinig wer's erlebt, der glaubt daran und
     weiss nicht wie…
     Da steht der Bub, und da steh' ich,
     und mit dem fremden Mädel dort
     wird er so glücklich sein, als wie halt Männer
     das Glücklichsein verstehen.'

STAN: That's Kraut, I know. What is it? What you were
     listening to?

REGINE: Three women, singing together, right? One,
     older, the Marschallin, the other two younger.

71

The Marschallin is renouncing the boy she loves. But as you watch this great cascade of love spurring out like the thunderous spray of a vast waterfall of heartbreak, comes this *sound*. But you know it's three *women*. The love of women, the love of woman for woman, the love of love itself and life. Continuing and replenishing the earth. Only they, the true fruit and proper multiplies. The fruit of a tree yielding seed. Listen, if you can tear yourself away from Smash Deel. (*She turns up the record player again.*) This is the Marschallin, the older one, watching her young lover with his betrothed: (*Pause.*)
'Most things in this world are unbelievable when you hear about them.
But when they happen to you, you believe them, and don't know why –
There stands the boy and here I stand, and with that strange girl
He will be as happy as any man knows how to be...'
(*She turns it off.*) Isn't that sublime?

STAN: Yes.

REGINE: Vulgar and sublime as only woman can achieve. She renounces the thing she loves the most: Octavian, orders, her life, her heart, to go to his bride.

STAN: Was it written by a man?

REGINE: Two men, overbearing Viennese pigs. Strauss and Von Hofmannsthal.

STAN: What, the Blue Danube geezer? He *could* have been a woman.

REGINE: Richard not Johann. He *was* a soppy man. You should read their letters to each other.

STAN: What, were they pouves?

REGINE: No. It's a lesson of two men trying to collaborate.

STAN: Like Morecambe and Wise?

REGINE: Do you know what he said, forty years later when some American soldiers broke into his house at the end of the war? They demanded: 'Who are you?' And he replied: 'I am the author of *Der Rosenkavalier!*'

STAN: That must have stumped them. Who's this Rosy Cavalier? How'd he treat *his* wife?

REGINE: Abominably.

STAN: But don't they, the audience, know it's a bird in drag?

REGINE: Of course they do, dolt! But they don't *feel* it. They feel them as three women, resplendent in their bodies and star-pointing female voices.

STAN: Didn't Shakespeare do that?

REGINE: But everyone knows Rosalind and Viola are an oafish Elizabethan's hairy idea of what they want a woman to be: poor imitation men. I'll take you to see it one day.

STAN: Thanks.

REGINE: I often wonder if Mozart wasn't a woman.

STAN: Wasn't he called Wolfgang? Good name for a group. Not bad – Wolfgang…

(*He pronounces it WOLF.*)

REGINE: His sister, his Constanze. *He* understood women. Ach, Constanze! All his women were like sisters. Look what fools men are: Almaviva pillaging and bullying for the privilege of his enslaved maidenheads; Figaro himself; Papageno – pathetic; Leperello, notching up the count of brutal seductions on his master's belted so-called manhood. The belt of young girl's slavery and gullibility; and Don Giovanni, that *arch* pretender! Squalid rides into town, cowboy cocksman, penile gangster. He got *his* St Valentine's Day all right, bootlegging his crabs and disease and sad seed all over civilisation. They've all got their St Valentine's Day coming to them, this blight of the world's Casanovas. A quick, sharp burst from all over the earth; from every girl from the North Side, the South Side, the West Side, the East Side.

STAN: Thought St. Valentine's Day was for lovers. Why, I sent you a card once.

REGINE: Very sweet of you, darling. But misguided in these times.

STAN: I see Smash Deel's number two in the charts.

REGINE: Yes, he mustn't start to slide. He's coming here today.

STAN: What – Smash? Cor! Can I see him?

REGINE: You will. You'll be busy with your camera and tapes.

REGINE: Appropriate phrase. Oh, yes, she's very militant.

STELLA: I hate those angelic little, well-brushed dirty little devils. Church propaganda for the innocence of man in his youth. Two of them jumped on me and ripped my gym-slip off and all but raped me.

REGINE: Poor girl. Well, get on, Stan. Oh, this is my er –

STELLA: Hullo, Mr – er – Frimley.

STAN: Way out, Miss Shrift.

STELLA: Way out? Does he mean hanging out?

REGINE: He's always catching up with last year's *Melody Maker*. Well, get on, Stan. And don't forget that key.

STAN: Right. See you, Miss Shrift.

STELLA: I'll be breathless.

(*He goes out.*)

REGINE: Drink or tea?

STELLA: Nothing, thanks. I may not stay long.

REGINE: I think you will. Sit down, darling. Anywhere. You can go, Wain. Keep an eye out for the other guests. (*He goes.*)

STELLA: I may not be able to stay, as I say. I might look in at the Hunt Ball Fashion Show. Sure to be a drag but the readers like a bit of how-the-other-half-lives. Especially the upper classes or their hunt followers and hangers-on fooling about with champagne; old-clothes couturiers turning the place into a flunkey's bazaar for nancy photographers and the general debs' drugs.

REGINE: I said the Vicar's wife was militant but not on *your* scale of power and influence. Don't they – I mean those sweaty men in El Vino, or whatever it is, call you the Black Fleet Street Rose?

STELLA: Not to my *face*. Now, what do you want from me? Not a polite country-house guest.

REGINE: What I think we'd both like.

STELLA: Which is what?

REGINE: I think *I* will have a drink. Do you mind?

STELLA: Be your guest.

REGINE: Rather a long stay.

STELLA: Not too long, I hope. My stuff's short and to the point. That's my house style.

(*REGINE fixes herself a drink while STELLA cases the room.*)

REGINE: Now, Stella… do you mind if I call you Stella?

STELLA: Thousands do. Quite a place you have here. Stables and grooms too, I see.

REGINE: I've always liked to live in the manner I'm accustomed – especially in the country.

STELLA: Were you always accustomed to such gracious living?

REGINE: Not on anything like this scale. But I always followed country pursuits eagerly.

STELLA: I'm sure. And got pursued for it.

REGINE: And then my late husband loved the country. He was Joint Master.

STELLA: Quite a nice cut off the joint all round. I shouldn't think Stan goes in for these – pursuits. Or girl grooms?

REGINE: (*STELLA couldn't put her down.*) He's always busy. He shouts a bit, goes to the races, a bit of photography – not for magazines –

STELLA: No. Home movies?

REGINE: Yes. Quite recently that. Oh, and he's very interested in pop. He managed a group for a while.

STELLA: Name?

REGINE: The Wheelwrights was one. Then I think it was The Vendetta.

STELLA: Doesn't ring a bell.

REGINE: Not much with me either. But he's very keen on 'young people'. I can't say I am myself. I don't think youth is its own reward any more than virtue. Being young in itself is hardly an achievement. Any more than having brown hair. I never liked young people when I was a 'young people' myself. But then he likes clichés, which is what young people are, of course.

STELLA: You couldn't read newspapers without them.

REGINE: Nobody would understand them then, would they? But I'm afraid Stan is a bit of a cliché himself, wide open to popular fashion. I suppose people who *are* clichés must be certain to learn others, even in their speech. He doesn't talk a lot but when he does I often

don't understand him at all. He even uses ones he doesn't
understand.

STELLA: Like?

REGINE: Oh, he understands the usual ones: like – funky;
cool it – I think that's out – ; bad trips; being in some
sort of 'scene' – sounds like a part in a play to me;
having hangups – he has lots of those I believe; chicks,
birds, calling everyone 'baby'; saying 'fucking' because
he doesn't know any other adjectives – or hardly;
chart-buster; he's picked up some he doesn't grasp at
all from some of the girls with social consciences, in
particular. Oh, you know the sort of thing: street action
groups; committee jargon; lobbying the council; even
'growing resentment' – you might read that in *The Times*
even; play communities, play centres, play groups,
centres for; centres of *all* kinds from 'pig bashing' to
'aggro' and 'agit-prop'; playgrounds, parks; talking about
his groups as if they were the Amadeus Quartet...

STELLA: Seems to me you don't like many things.
Including Stan.

REGINE: Oh, but I do. I don't believe in hiding one's
malice. I like women and some men; sex now and then,
preferably in private; horses –

STELLA: Naturally.

REGINE: – some dogs, most cats; champagne, chip butties,
Guinness; oysters, gulls' eggs; opera, stand-up comics –
not drag acts though; some older homosexuals; Jane
Austen not Conrad; a certain religiosity if it's comic
enough; silver – you might like to see my collection;
motor bikes, roller-skating and, still, I'm afraid, Monte
Carlo; rock and roll if it's the older, more primitive sort;
Hell's Angels. Oh, I can't think...

STELLA: A picture emerges.

REGINE: Oh, hate crosswords, chess and bridge and all the
people who like them.

STELLA: You seem to like mirrors too, I see.

REGINE: Adore them. Even when I look awful, which is
most of the time.

STELLA: For what you see *in* them? Or through them?
Come, Lady Frimley, you didn't invite me all the way
down here to give an interview. We're not each
other's scene.

REGINE: I think we *might* be.

STELLA: Look, let's get down to it. I may still have to go
to the huntin', shootin', fashion show. Is it true what
I hear that you run a call-girls' establishment for randy,
big-name weekenders?

REGINE: Yes.

STELLA: Right. Now what do you want?

REGINE: Don't you want what Evelyn Waugh called
a scoop?

STELLA: Listen, Lady Frimley, I know you think you're
something of a two-way personality smart-ass. But I don't
think you're a fool. Some sort of kooky revolutionary,
classic English eccentric – which you couldn't be.
Oh, yes, I've looked around about you.

REGINE: Naturally. How professional of you.

STELLA: Don't play games with me. I know them all and
the rules, even the ones to break. All right, we all know
you're a phoney. Name, background, publishers, the lot.
You're not thirty-eight and you're a Jewish girl from
Hackney with a goodish plastic surgeon. And your name
is Myra Steinitz.

REGINE: Right. Absolutely. Every detail. Nice of you not
to mention my other marriages. Still, they're fairly
common knowledge. No, you see, I am something of a
cliché myself.

STELLA: So then: what's the set up here?

REGINE: Well, it's not quite what you imagine. I think
it's a trifle more sophisticated, both in function and
intention. It *is* what you say – in a few column inches
that is to say. Yes, the mirrors *are* two way. What insights
into life 'as it is really lived' the profession of journalism
gives a young girl – as time goes on. I have been
running this 'place', if you like, for quite some time.
Quite long enough for me, and if as you say, there are

already rumours about it where you come from, it's high
time to pack up the operation and plan for the next and
most important stage.

STELLA: And that is?

REGINE: Oh, some sort of frolicsome revolution or
simple old shit hitting the world's fan. I have run this
'establishment', if that's the word, to have enticed
almost every man in England.

STELLA: I don't believe it. Men always cover up. And in
their numbers there's safety. How ever many have you
got? You know there are scoops and scoops; the law
of libel.

REGINE: English libel. An old dog in his corner of the
world. There's the *world* press. German magazines,
French ones, Dutch, Swedish television companies,
America. Russia. I've got quite a missile here, as an
American general said to me once.

STELLA: Go on.

REGINE: This makes Watergate three-day cricket for
baboons. I've got film, thousands of MILES of it.
And with what a cast. Well, all the obvious ones, I
needn't tell you. Parliament. I didn't know we had so
many members. Sorry, but it did seem more than six
hundred. Judiciary, of course. Press but enough and not
more. Civil Service, Armed Service. Royals.
Footballers. Daft ones, gay ones, rotten ones,
distinguished. Oh yes, the Church, but they don't count
for much. Tapes, stills. Too much material, of course.
But used superbly. We can't make it so all-embracing
that everyone will yawn and get down to it themselves.
What we need is a superb team; team, yes, of directors,
Eisensteins, Orson Welleses, John Fords, to put it all
together. A sort of works of Shakespeare, Ivan the
Terrible in epic parts. How does it begin to strike you?

STELLA: Interesting.

REGINE: Remember. Think of us. Us. Women. Half the
world. That rocked the cradle could bring down the chop
for all time. Or long enough.

STELLA: As simple as that?

REGINE: As all discoveries of genius. Banally simple.
Like Leonardo, the wheel, iron weapons, the workers
overthrowing the *ancien régime*. And the *régime* is
certainly *ancien,* I'm sure you'd be the first to agree.
Pure organisation. Apparently, again, too true for the
words of even the simple clichés of Stan. *I* recreate a
very English cliché. The Country Weekend. This is the
Garsington of Lechery – instead of Literature.

STELLA: Garsington?

REGINE: Garsington. It was the rather spinsterish, on all
sides, world of Ottoline Morrell. The world of Asquith,
Keynes, Duncan Grant, Virginia Woolf and Leonard,
Lawrence –

STELLA: I know. I know. I don't just read newspapers,
you know.

REGINE: All very respectable. Waspish witticism and
music and banjos and economics, flirtations and politics.
People can't flirt any more, can they? Pity; I enjoyed it
once. Saved you from all that thrashing about after and
perspiration and excuses and making calls from phone
boxes instead of your house. All quite different from
your mustachioed Edwardian adultery festivals and the
Countess of Warwick and bedroom keys and nightgowns
and brandyport filled men slipping down those long,
cold corridors to the heavy warmth of another's heaving
feather four-poster.

STELLA: What have you got apart from thousands of miles
of unedited film and so on?

REGINE: Stars, you mean: oh, about a thousand of what
used to be called pillars of society, paragons of
public life.

STELLA: Simple. You get the stars and the equipment.
What about the girls?

REGINE: Fresh picked. To them it doesn't matter. If they
go along with the principle, they've nothing to lose.
They're the heroes. They caught out the cancer. They'll be
the Provos of Womanhood all over the world.

STELLA: Maybe the *other* women won't buy it.

REGINE: They will. They'll have to. *You* know the way it's
    going. And in such a short time. The star is in the
    firmament. And it shines for *us*. The revolution *will*
    come. Then we'll see. It'll find its Robespierre.
STELLA: And you its Danton?
REGINE: I've had a good life. I expect it to be better, for a
    while, at least.
STELLA: Where's all this vast production-script?
REGINE: In the bank vaults. Stan does that. He'll do
    anything for money. To him it's just a new cliché of
    history. Like 1066, 1789 or 1914 – if he knows *them*.
    (*STELLA pauses for thought.*)
    Your presence. This must be the last weekend. You could
    be our link with 'the media' (cliché). Stay and see what
    you feel. It'll be more rewarding than the Hunt Ball
    Fashion Show.
STELLA: (*Intrigued now.*) Tell me some more.
REGINE: This is the time to *strike*. We've got all we need.
    First, the girls will come. I'll brief you on them but
    I doubt you'll need it. The men you'll know about.
STELLA: So you think the soldier's pole is about to fall,
    pulled by *you*? You see, I do know my Shakespeare.
    I wonder. Like all these things. Some will like it.
    Some will hate it. There's one thing for certain, Regine.
    There's no going back.
REGINE: Welcome, my friend. As you say, there's no
    going back. We don't need to draw in any more if we
    don't want to. We're the girls' Jesuits. Give us a girl for
    the first of her grooming, her indoctrination, and I'll
    make her first a whore and then her whole self, her *self*
    for life. The prick is just where it is. The cunt is where
    the heart lies.
STELLA: Yes, all that shit about envy. Who'd envy *that*!
REGINE: Yes, it helps them in their endless romanticism
    about you. His balls are where his brains should be.
    That's why he used up what his mettle should be.
    Lyrical poetry, desire failing, laments for lost love,
    inaccessible troubadour mistresses without a servant.
    If only they knew how they sickened us with their

schooldays, memories, endless, endless memories. Their peacock regimentals, their desperate fetishes and paltry pornography. Why? They are hollow, empty wooden horses all dressed up or undressed with nowhere in the universe to go. No Troy to infiltrate let alone *penetrate*. And what you said about envy. Envy! My God.

STELLA: (*Getting exhilarated.*) No wonder the Victorians in their wisdom voted for fig leaves. David. Greek gods. Ugh! A schoolgirl's giggle round the V and A. It was true aesthetic judgement, not a moral one.

REGINE: See it dangle, dingle dangle, jingle jangle in its usual petulant pendulance. A sorry, blue-veined pork sword looking like an unripe, yellowish Stilton. Lying against its horse-hair sack, wee bag, of a million million pestilent tadpoles looking for a muddy pool to rest in. Throbbing for all the world's distaste like a turkey's gobbling neck.

STELLA: No wonder they call it a 'gobble job'.

REGINE: Erect, well now, *that's* a sight, if they can get it up without your thumbs splitting and fingers inflamed with corns, more horn than they could ever manage with *that*. Erect as an Irish volunteer, blind, hopeless, eyeless in girls' Gaza. These footling frail inches of phallus, trying to ascend Everest like a Mick navvy without enough scaffolding.

STELLA: Perhaps *that's* what Disraeli meant by 'the greasy pole of politics'.

REGINE: Rather keen on poles, aren't they? Well, that flag won't fly much longer. It's coming down. In all its tatters and tyranny. *We* will be the mast, the mast, mast of woman, flying *our* flag. Greasy indeed! Mrs Disraeli must have known the real truth behind that bit of front bench grandiloquence.

STELLA: And their awful *jokes*. You can imagine the stuff *I* have to listen to, Black Rose or not.

REGINE: Men invented bordellos, but women perfected the running of them.

STELLA: Like *you*! I *will* have a drink, after all. We'll drink to the weekend. To the revolution. To the scaffold agleam with male unreconstituting blood.

REGINE: Here's to us all.

STELLA: (*Relaxed now.*) This joke, this journalist who called me Black Rose because I wasn't having his whisky head snoring on my breast. He told me this. Supposed to be sophisticated and male fun. Right? Ready?

REGINE: Ready. If you tell it well, I warn you, I might –

STELLA: They hate us because we can't *tell* jokes. Should be cut like a good jacket. No joins. All that stuff. *Male* joke! In this case Red-nosed Rose of Yorkshire. Bugsy meets Louie. That's right. You see, I can tell it to you, like my hairdresser. Bugsy says to Louie, say, Louie, you're looking great. Great. Why it's years since I seen you. (*All in gangster accent.*) Must be, what, eight – eight years. Yeah. Long stretch. Say, where you living now? Florida. Great. Miami Beach. Suits you. You look great. Great. Say, whatever happened to that little broad – er, chick – girl you were so keen on? What was her name? Rochelle. That's right. Great kid. Gee, Louie, you're looking great. Say, whatever happened to – er her, Rochelle... I *married* her... Married her, married her, but that's great, Louie. Really great. Say, how is she, Louie... She's dead. (How'm I doing?)

REGINE: Great.

STELLA: Dead! But, Louie, that's terrible, that's awful! Gee, Louie... What'd, what she die of...? CRABS... Crabs! Jesus Christ, Louie, people don't die of CRABS...
They do if they give 'em to me.
(*She gives an imitation of George Reft with his cigar.*)

REGINE: I *told* you I'd laugh at one *of your* jokes. Even at one of – those. The point is there's a General Amin in man bursting, brown or white, to get out. 'Ah'm a good marksman.' So he can make twelve piccaninnies.

STELLA: All that rigidity. The fact is men don't want to die so much they won't be born, so foetus themselves up in music halls, clubs, regiments and pubs. Do you know

what that Yorkshire git said to me when he knew he
wasn't going to get it and was too pissed to remember
where he'd left it? He said, as if he were Voltaire,
morality is the child of imagination, which is why
women don't have it. That we'd had more leisure than
most to paint, sing, play the piano, write poetry, verses,
novels, music. What did we get: the Brontës and the Ivy
Benson Band. That not women invented steam and God
but US!

REGINE: How ignorant. (*Slightly sending up STELLA's
new fervour.*)

STELLA: Barefoot and pregnant. Even sweet-natured
Chekhov said women didn't have a baby every *day.* Just
every year. Fable about Barefoot and poorly shod. I don't
think sweet Doctor Chekhov would have bought you any
shoes at all. As your cliché book would say, marriage
needs re-phrasing.

REGINE: We're in total agreement. But don't you see that's
the point. We all are. To us. To us women.

STELLA: Right.

REGINE: To us.

STELLA: To us.

REGINE: (*Toast.*) The aim, the aim is *not* social equality, no,
it's not that, it's social DISHARMONY. All they have is
an inexhaustible crop of regrets. Regrets!

STELLA: *They* like the language of concealment. Not us.

REGINE: We're going to enjoy this, Stella. This is the
barricades. At last.

STELLA: Barricades! Here we come! We're closing your
borderline. Like going into the EEC, it filled a long,
unfelt want. Now we don't want *you*!

REGINE: You know that chap Aretino or something like
that. I just went to Farley Road Secondary School till
I was fourteen. Well, it seems this old character *laughed
himself* to death at a dirty joke. *Just* like my old man.
So did I nearly. Thank God *I* didn't. Think of all that
money. Only time he made me laugh.
(*They both giggle.*)

85

We've got a whole spotlight of dignitaries and here come the last of the bombs. Lead 'em on!

(*WAIN comes in.*)

WAIN: Mrs Pangborn is here, m'lady.

REGINE: Give me a minute and then show her in.

WAIN: Very well, m'lady.

STELLA: Letitia Pangborn?

REGINE: Who else? Publishers' parties and lays all round, grand Tory MP husband, writes books on the cookery of sex, travel (over-researched), popular biographies. Regrets, like so many, she hadn't been an actress and set the world alight without the benefit of rich husband, large ears and hungry little typewriter to feed for fame and a reputation for beauty *and* intellect...

STELLA: Wheel 'em on.

WAIN: (*Enters.*) Mrs Pangborn, m'lady.

(*MRS PANGBORN is pretty, confident, about the same age as the rest.*)

REGINE: Darling! I'm so glad you're *first*. You know all the ropes. Only I've got a rather funny little lady coming next and I may have to sort her out a bit. You know Stella, don't you?

LETITIA: Yes. Hullo.

STELLA: It's all right. You've nothing to worry about from me.

REGINE: No. She's one of us.

STELLA: Yes. Not just an outside observer. A participant. A resistance worker. Not soon enough, alas. I could have helped.

REGINE: It was my one insight. It's nice to have *one*. Drink?

LETITIA: Thanks. Not before work. Who have you got for me?

REGINE: Stratford West.

LETITIA: Oh, not him. That awful, creepy show-biz journalist. Why do you always get me journalists?

REGINE: Sorry.

LETITIA: Don't be. I was just complaining.

REGINE: Well, poor Stratford can only get plastic starlets

to roll in his garden before he goes back to the wife and kids in Ealing. Pretending he's been living it up – for the paper – to all hours. And he *wants* a bit of class and intellect. He can't spell 'existentialism' but he'll swoon when you bite it into his grizzled old ears.

LETITIA: Isn't it time we closed up shop? You must have enough to wreck the entire Western Civilisation.

REGINE: That's exactly what we've agreed. With Stella.

LETITIA: Thank God. I'm sick to death of staring up at myself in the ceiling mirror. I almost fancy my husband. But the House is too busy having divisions these days.

REGINE: You can always go back to publishing.

LETITIA: That's like going back as an old girl when you were once Head Girl.

REGINE: How's the writing?

LETITIA: I wish you wouldn't ask silly questions to people like writers, Regine. You should know better. It's like asking a window cleaner 'How are the windows then?' It's the same as usual. It's all hours but I get it done. In spite of Tom and the children.

REGINE: Well, you *are* rich.

LETITIA: *He* is. Thank God.

REGINE: I've explained the set-up to Stella. She not only understands but she's right behind us.

LETITIA: Good. We'll need all the help we can get. These men will think of *something*. That's what worries us.

STELLA: With your bottom in the air, your pants hanging down in a frightened animal way, it'll be difficult to think of anything. Privacy's never really been assaulted and brought down. They won't know what hit them or why anyone could do it to them. *Their* God will have cast *them* out. *We'll* be left laughing.

LETITIA: In Paradise? No men!

REGINE: We'll make our own paradise. Our own kind of men. And remake God's bad job on the whole unfortunate incident. We will multiply. We have already. That's what it meant.

LETITIA: I hope so. I can't *stay*, Regine. I'm sorry. Tom's wanting me on his constituency stint this weekend.

STELLA: Last time.

REGINE: As I said, I've this funny little woman –

(*WAIN comes in.*)

WAIN: Mrs Sands, m'lady.

REGINE: Send her in.

(*WAIN goes out.*)

Be nice to her. She must be very nervous.

(*WAIN enters with MRS ISOBEL SANDS. She is shrewd-looking but nervous. However, making a go of it. Late thirties. Quite attractive. Not startlingly dressed. WAIN goes out.*)

REGINE: Mrs Sands! Isobel, right? Isobel, this is Letitia Pangborn, Stella Shrift – she shows no shrift and gives no favour – I expect you've heard of her?

ISOBEL: Yes. Of course.

(*They exchange the usual things and sit.*)

REGINE: Isobel, anything, no? Isobel, this won't be too difficult for you. These people are close friends and I've heard from many sources what an honest kind of character you are. We can be frank. If you want to change your mind at any time, of course you may. I'll understand. I just wanted someone quite honest, well, decent, who was intelligent and curious and in some distress but in control; objective but emotional, who would get in on this – just for once, and form her judgements for herself of what we have all created for ourselves.

ISOBEL: There's no danger of that. I shall stay as long as you need me.

REGINE: Wonderful. Well, to cases: there will be about five or six women here and about seven men. So some may have to do overtime.

STELLA: Jog. She's a sperm vampire.

REGINE: Could you tell me a bit more about yourself?

ISOBEL: Not much really. I've been married nearly twenty years. I've three teenage children who don't take notice of either of us much. They really scare both of us now and I suppose we avoid them most of the time and they us... I feel young and I seem to have no future. Although, I *feel,* perhaps stupidly, it might be not new but *different.* I don't know...

REGINE: I know.

ISOBEL: I do know I reduce him to such despair and tedium, he dreads coming in and I dread his key in the lock.

REGINE: Don't worry. The stars are pointing for all of us. I've well, teamed you, if you don't mind the expression, with Leonard Grimthorpe.

ISOBEL: One's free. But for what. (*Pause.*) I'm sorry for him. And he for me. (*Pause.*) He really goes pale and damp with fear and irritation with me. I can watch it. It's like a boiling migraine. You need to put him to bed in the dark, alone as long as possible. While I sit and stare at nothing, well, our house walls; the walls of our house.

REGINE: Isobel. Let me get you a drink. I have to be practical I'm afraid. I have to be speedy and generalise because time is pressing on us a bit. *Len Grimthorpe*: he's decided not to be brilliant because he couldn't bear it. He really does, I think, I think he does, he believes in the beauty of failure. Not just as a literary throw-away for someone like Hindle to seize on.

STELLA: Who's got *him*?

REGINE: You have.

STELLA: Oh, no. Not *two* journalists.

REGINE: Usual enough. Anyway, all this bedroom placement is very difficult. *You* try it. You'll probably have Smash Deel first.

STELLA: No. I think I'm resigning.

REGINE: It's only the once, Stella. And you are new. We've all done our bit.

STELLA: What about Mrs Sands?

REGINE: No, I don't think she could handle Smash Deel.

STELLA: Quick flick of the wrist.

REGINE: I think he'll take a lot more than that. He's a wrist breaker.

ISOBEL: I'm very athletic. Yes, I know you're grinning. But I don't need, I don't want to be protected.

REGINE: This is my placement. It took hours to work out and I'm sticking to it. Otherwise, we'll all argue and be here all night and no customers. (*To ISOBEL.*) Now Len is an odd fish. But he can be fun. And he won't ask too much of you. Because he expects so little. I see you're wearing tights.

ISOBEL: Oh, are they – ?

REGINE: But the last time Len came he complained of someone – I can't remember who – wearing tights. He said they were for men not women. For male dancers and Shakespearian actors. He couldn't stand that patchy triangle round the centre. Definitely underwear, I'm afraid. I'll get it laid out in your room. I know what he likes. Quite harmless and dull. Totally *MALE*. Do *we* think of such things?

ISOBEL: Right. I'll remember. I wasn't sure.

REGINE: He's much more full of gaiety than he sounds. I think you might get on. I can't quite think quite why I asked him. He's not really famous. Sort of well known. For doing nothing – much. But quite good at it. (*WAIN enters.*)

WAIN: Lady Gwen Mitchelson and Miss Jog Fienberg.

REGINE: Two minutes, Wain. Show them the new conservatory.
(*He goes, nodding.*)
Lady Gwen: like me, a girl from Hackney. I knew her at school. Another nibbling girl-actress who went to Hollywood too late but brought it back to Weybridge or somewhere. Lots of alimony from sweet, misguided ex-husband actor who has given her two children, a mansion by-Californian-standards in Malibu. Lives off him and their accumulated houses and pictures and furniture. Remarried title and some money. Bad type for *us*. But ideal man bait. For the right type. And there are plenty. Jog – yes, Jog *Fienberg*; US nutcase. Wants all men to have compulsory vasectomy with or without the option of the death penalty. Now, she is a cliché. Except that you won't believe her when you see her. Don't listen, that's all. Above all, don't argue. Useful because she does all the donkey work.
(*JOG and Lady GWEN enter.*)

Gwen, darling! Jog.

(*They fit her description. GWEN has clearly taken hours to prepare herself. JOG is in jeans and sweater and badly, really badly in need of a bath.*)

You do make a quite splendid pair! I think you all more or less know –

(*They go through the pantomime of introductions.*)

Drink? Ah, Coke for Jog.

GWEN: No, thanks.

REGINE: Not dieting again. It's so *oppressive*. Like your eyelashes and wigs. People who diet are like converts to warmed-up religious beliefs. And your lovely rich husband, and various children by which of them and your home? How *is* your home? The Ranch Style one in Mill Hill? Or have you moved?

GWEN: It's all great. So where are the guys?

REGINE: We're waiting for Rachel.

GWEN: Oh, the Countess of Bleak. She never really made it, did she? Couldn't act. Write. Anything. No good in the sack.

REGINE: Well, they do say that every cigar-smoking gentleman having lunch at the Black Rhinoceros has known the favours of both of you or either.

GWEN: Darling, if I didn't know you so well and had nothing better to do for an hour or so, I'd go straight back to London.

REGINE: Don't worry; this is the last of the weekends.

GWEN: Thank God! It takes so long to get here. And you know how suspicious Mitch gets.

REGINE: Next week is Bastille Day.

GWEN: What day? Here, I hope you're not going to go *too* far.

STELLA: We're all in this and you more than most. You compounded the system. With your make-up and Beverly Hills in Virginia Water; and film premières but no proper films; your alimony; your calculations; your shop-girl vanities. Just get on with being what you are and always have been; a prissy producer's tart with smart solicitors and accountants. You're not *unknown*, you know.

GWEN: Thanks. I don't need *you.*

STELLA: Watch it, you untalented trollop. I can get you
eaten up. A threat like that from me, of all people,
wouldn't intimidate little pussy. But it will *you.* Because,
beneath all that British Beverly Hills, you're more of a
cliché than you are and what you write about.

REGINE: And you Jog.

JOG: Is this the last one? I hope so. I can't stand another
man, the sight of one. The mother-homemaker-secretary
kind is still what they want, want, and they won't believe
we're not. Who wants their prick rights? All laying
down this crap. All stewing maleness and rhetoric.
What are we, tits and no mind, to them? We are, we are
the politics. The gags are better, they're better, not much
but anything's better than what – they – call themselves
– straights. Straight. What's straight? In this world. Men?
Straight. I'll never go again with any man. We all know
what they end up *doing* to you! Sweet Jesus! Not *man,*
Jesus! Give us, give us a woman for President! Is it
possible? Couldn't it be? (*She weeps a little.*)

STELLA: You're not all that interesting, Jog.

JOG: Great. So tell me how uninteresting I am. I want
a lover and it isn't a man and it isn't a woman.
I'm a soldier, a fighter, I'm an academic, I'm educated
middle-class American and you all, you English, look
down from your sinking, stinking rat shit at us... Help
the woman who is obliged to work in any patriarchal,
cultural set-up. A reunification of the reverence of
the female principle. Give us the Goddess. Dig the
Goddesses. Diana, Mary, Penelope. You have wasted us.
Wasted us. We *are* your waste. Your effluent. Men and
their things. Big deal. Big fucking deal. Let them do it
to themselves. You're all a Big Deal. Protagonists.
Tyrants. *We* are the killers now. Kill them. Kill the men.
Before we do it. To ourselves. We're so scared. Kick out
the fags too. Kill them all.

REGINE: Wain will get you some coffee.

JOG: What are we fucking well waiting for? You say I'm
a cliché, don't you? Well, what do you think you are?

REGINE: The same as you. As all of us...
(*She rings the bell. WAIN enters.*)
Some coffee for Miss Fienberg. And anyone else.
WAIN: Yes, m'lady. The Countess of Bleak is here.
REGINE: Send her in at once. We're late.
(*He nods and goes out.*)
The Countess of Bleak. Another disjointed actress, married into the aristocracy from the usual disappointment and cupidity... I'm afraid you have to bait for the big fish with almost unspeakable morsels. If that's what gulls them. And it usually does.
(*They all look depressed in the extreme. WAIN re-enters with RACHEL, the Countess of Bleak.*)
WAIN: The Countess of Bleak.
REGINE: Darling. Anything? Sure, right, we'll start off.
(*To WAIN.*) Let the gentlemen in as they arrive. Oh, you know the batting order.
WAIN: Yes, m'lady.
REGINE: Well, how are the Bleaks?
RACHEL: Bloody mean and petty as ever for seven centuries.
REGINE: Now, I think we're all here... You know why we're all here. Make bait and it's time to strike, haul up the nets and trawl in those wriggling creatures you've had to bear with in all this time. Jog, you've got, oh, I'm so confused now, I think you've drawn Smash Deel.
JOG: Kill him!
REGINE: And – I – think – Ashley Withers. Newspaper proprietor. Not Stella's but a well, BIG, little deal. Now, quick briefing: Stella, you've got Hindle. You know the score, you know him.
STELLA: Don't I just! They *all* do.
REGINE: Well, as I say, ladies, this will be our last weekend. I don't need to say much to you. Even our newcomer, Mrs Sands, seems more than capable of holding her own – if you'll forgive the linguistic handstands of the good old English language. Even if some grandparents leapt off the boat from Omsk or Tomsk. I'll just add a few general things. As I say, Stella,

you know Hindle, but he might stray, and they *do*
sometimes, elsewhere –

STELLA: Hope so.

REGINE: Well, ladies, Hindle Nates is a famous ex-boy
wonder from Oxford – I can't remember which college –
who writes about almost anything for anyone and makes
a great deal of money doing it. He has been trying to
cultivate style ever since he was seen wearing lilac
knickers and a top hat on Magdalen Bridge on his way to
the Union reading Marx in a loud falsetto. He stunned
the single-minded students, who've talked about it ever
since and tickled some of the dons. He became a 'legend'
in that city of dreaming spires and sure of soft jobs for
its dud comics. He likes Wagner, anything American
or clearly ephemeral, as well as dangerously painful
spanking. So watch for that. He hates the past, even
yesterday, with almost pathological hatred. And even
today is a broken series of disappointments. You have to
look like tomorrow's girl even if you feel like the
forgotten or unfashionable decades of the century.
So mind your bottoms, ladies. They can get very stripey
and sore after half an hour with Hindle in the quest for
his undergraduate glory. He writes unbelievably
vindictive, incomprehensible, apparently erudite letters
to obscure journals like the *Listener* which specialise
in vindictiveness. So give him a bit of politics and
literature. You don't need to say anything interesting or
know who or what you're talking about. In fact, if you
sound like Marilyn Monroe giving her views on
Kierkegaard, he'll be perspiring with joy and discovery.
A lot of what I say applies, in principle, to all our *other*
guests. Their interests are all there to be titivated of
whatever kind. But Hindle is quite a good example even
if he's a bit over the usual intellectual top. As always,
just drop a few names and he'll say something which
he'll attribute to *you*. After all, he's grateful for the other
services you're dealing out... It never does any harm to
pretend you like mostly plays by Negroes or Irishmen
on the run for murder. Women's Lib tolerated, often

welcomed by the 'bondage' artists. You can even pretend you're gay, which can spur some of them on. If you are indeed gay, it may be even helpful if it turns them off and it saves time and labour. They may, as often, think you're secretly longing, yes, here we go, to be *dominated*, yes, dominated by them, particularly if he's an established genius or today's idea of paradise and tomorrow's sexual garbage. You can offer him pot. Some will pretend to be in *that* scene. But most won't bother. You're safe with theatre chat because no one knows anything about it and cares less. Cinema is more dodgy because some of them are practically archivists and, anyway, it often digs deep into their grubby schoolboy consciousness. Say the Theatre is dead – as always – except the Fringe or Underground. You don't need to have *seen* any. *They* won't have seen any either. Or they'll have fallen asleep. Talk about non-happening happenings being the *ultimate* and so on. You don't have to *explain*. Just *say* it casually. Talk a lot of off-hand filth in between as if you were doing that brushing your glowing spring of hair from your clear fountainhead forehead. Just, oh, just be generally *charmless* is fairly good standard behaviour. But watch it if it misfires. Then, be gentle, loving, attentive. If you've got stubble in your armpits, say jolly things which will intrigue his running-down tape-recorder mind, desperately trying to freeze each new experience to release all the lost, shattered ones. So he'll tell you – a bit usually. Try not to actually bore him but let's simply hope he won't notice either ante or post coitum. It may be *triste est* quite often or just like getting up from a sauna and massage. There's always something he'll be interested in. Find it and he'll do the talking. Otherwise be enigmatic. Easiest thing in the world. Shut your mouth and look sulky. A few crass judgements may, on the other hand, make him feel good. Don't be *really* funny. That's poaching *his* rights. Oh, you can say – I'm sorry to be repetitive. *You* all know your stuff but I have to try and make you feel a bit enthusiastic about this *dismal* project. Remember it's the

last time over that timeless top and then a New World
waits for us! And we were the crack troops, who blew up
the world's idea of itself and what they once called
mankind. Womankind! And a time will come when we
can afford to be Women *and* kind – when it's just and
right. Anything else? Yes. Say you've written a book
called *Fucking Our Way to Revolution and Socialism.*
Some of you probably have for all I know. Say lightly
that Michael Foot is a right-wing fascist. It'll get some
sort of response, however drowsy. That Chairman Mao is
the Kung Fu of gradualism. Talk about going down –
with Man – or in any way. You'll find out what 'turns
him on'. Cliché but remember you are dealing with men;
and men who are the products of a society which turned
itself into an almost overnight cliché. Either way,
political action always sounds sexy because it means
you're violent and passionate even if brainless – so much
the better. Yes, you can say things like 'violence is the
greatest orgasm of Historical Experience and
Significance'. That'll do for right *or* left. I'm only talking
about the verbal aspects because it can often save you
from the exhausting contortions of great or famous men.
Anything you say about painting is more or less OK.
As long as it shows you've *heard* of it and have got
reasonable eyesight. Stately homes should be turned into
brothels like mine or abortion clinics; or pads for
squatters, drop-outs and the workers. Whoever they are
it'll amuse you with your perky flight of female mind.
Oh, as for sex, when you get to it: whatever he *wants* if
you can manage it without incurring physical damage.
Or try and talk him into something else. Lots of mouth-
work all round usually works so make sure you haven't
had rice pudding or spinach for lunch. If you wear
dentures, you can even turn it to advantage. While he's
luxuriating, toss off an odd *mot* like 'The Queen should
be buggered daily in the Palace Yard.' If you don't care
for the practice yourself think of something else that isn't
entirely repellent to you. There's always Princess Anne
and stallions. Anyone'll go for that. Just choose the least

objectionable lead to the action. Above all, be
spontaneous. That's the only real fun of it. Do a quick
sound out and *play* it. People are best at it – like women,
they're numinously intuitive. Drill into the ocean bed of
your feminine consciousness. Approve or disapprove.
Be disparaging or dismissive. Manically enthusiastic or
just moody and full of hidden hurt and failure. Men *love*
failure. Especially the ones who've made it early or easy.
Or you can be tantalisingly arcane. I have a lady who
always plays records by Wanda Landowska and talks for
ages about her in her midwife's skirt and her hands
poised like gentle hawks over the keyboard. Then she
says 'May I play you some of her Scarlatti?' She talks
about Japs – yes, just about the nastiest race on earth, so
that's imaginative – little dears calling to speckled deer
on their strange flutes. Then she has a record of Tibetan
monks chanting a fifteenth-century prayer to booming
bells. Then it's usually 'Ah, let's go back to England.
To Byrd'. You see she believes – or pretends to admire
and venerate anyone trying to put *significance* into their
or our lives. Significance! That's a good stopper.
Significance. It's a word that can't even signify. So use it
if you like it or it amuses you. It's true – I've miles of
her on film doing it. But it is significant…? To us. It's a
ball breaker. 'Now that the captains and the kings have
departed.' No, I won't tell you any more about her.
She has her own special star quality and she's no chicken
either. But what she's done for *us!* Quote unreadable
writers like Fanon, Lubin, Marx; be odd but withdrawn
about Sylvia Plath; bluff about Ted Hughes. If you really
can't stand the thought of it all, vomit. Only, take care –
he *may* like it. Eat it or something. Men like dirty talk
but not about the realities of women's insides so a lot of
banter about tubes and afterbirth and tubes and babies'
heads and legs and forceps and so on will send some
men, especially the nicer ones, really off to the
bathroom… Oh, but you will all use your own
techniques. Believe me, from what I've seen, the female
mind and body is a holy miracle of ingenuity and divine

invention. Blake has nothing on HER visions and explorations. That's why we're here. That's *the message.* Right? No questions?… On with the final engagement of Life, its very self…

(*WAIN enters.*)

WAIN: Mr Grimthorpe and Mr Deel are here, m'lady.

REGINE: Send them in. Ladies, we are about to re-enter Paradise. On our own terms. With or without men. Cheers.

(*They all toast. Enter LEONARD GRIMTHORPE and SMASH DEEL. LEONARD is not bad-looking, fortyish, slightly vague, something of an affection. SMASH is what you'd expect.*)

Leonard, how delightful of you to come after all.

LEONARD: Delighted I could make it.

REGINE: And Mr Deel. Smash – we've all been on edge for hours. Now, let's all get together. There'll be others here soon so we can have a while to get to know one another. You may even know some of us. We have to be careful. You know, ex-wives, people in politics or on newspapers.

LEONARD: I've no worries on any of those scores. But then I'm afraid I take all things as they come. Sorry, cliché first time.

REGINE: Don't worry, darling. We invent them down here. Mr Deel, do you know Miss Stella Shrift? Don't worry, she won't give *you* short shrift though that's her craft and very good she is at it, I think, don't you?

SMASH: Eh?

REGINE: Now, Leonard, who don't you know?

LEONARD: This lady to begin with.

REGINE: Ah, this is Mrs Isobel Sands, Leonard Grimthorpe. Like you, I don't believe she does anything in particular.

LEONARD: Good. Hullo…

ISOBEL: Hullo…

End of Act One.

ACT TWO

Scene 1

Scene exactly the same but now full with the new arrivals. These are ROBERT BIGLEY, a portly young millionaire developer; STRATFORD WEST, the show-biz correspondent referred to in the first Act; FREDERICK BLACK, a rather bored-looking impresario, clearly very rich; JOHN STEWKES, Tory back-bencher, rather like a lofty-looking suspicious lizard; finally, ASHLEY WITHERS, newspaper proprietor, a jolly, quick, intelligent man, older than most of the others. REGINE is trying to introduce them to the seated and lolling assembly. SMASH is listening to one of his own recordings at the back of the room.

REGINE: You'll have to sort it out for yourselves. But in
no particular batting order. This is Robert Bigley, the
one who rose from being the son of a self-made –
I never understand what 'self-made' means. We all *make*
ourselves. No. Perhaps you don't agree. Anyway, to
become a self-made millionaire himself. If you want to
come here by private plane or jet to Paris for lunch or
helicopter to your box at the Derby, *all* the Stewards'
enclosures of everything, Henley, Ascot, you name it…
Founders' Day, Cowes, he'll be there or get you there
quicker and better than anyone.

BIGLEY: I say, Regine, you *are* putting me down and no
mistake.

REGINE: You know I admire you irredeemably. I love
millionaires but if they're young it's beyond belief. This
is Stratford West.

WEST: Not to be compared with Stratford East.

REGINE: Darling, you *must* resist that joke. He's always
interviewing starlets hot from bosomy film premières.
Miss X – seen in all but the nude. 'Read what *she* says
about men and the older men in particular. She has been
a model and played parts in two television series' – yet
to be seen.

WEST: That means either they won't be seen or she played a maid or a one-line typist in both.

REGINE: So if you have any theatrical or film ambitions, Stratford's your man. He's also *very* delightful. This is Freddy Black, the impresario. Well, you all know him. Got four hits in the West End. Cases joints like Nottingham, Edinburgh, Bristol, Greenwich, the Royal Court, The Theatre In The Ground, The Theatre On The Roof, like a cat burglar, and transfers them immediately – if they get rave notices. Shrewd boy, Freddy. Never backs talent, just a talent for finding backers. Never spent a penny on a production in his life. *Another,* yet another young millionaire! Dear Freddy. The Transfer Dead-Certainty-Only King. *This* is John Stewkes, not a millionaire alas, but brilliant, an MP, but try to keep off politics because *he* won't. By the way, he's Tory but you needn't worry, he'll disagree with left *and* right. He's sort of left and right of the other circle. Or something like that.

STEWKES: No politics, I promise, Regine. You've just issued an open invitation to your usual insane lefties or your drabbest right-wingers.

REGINE: Don't you think he's a right dandy?

STEWKES: I've been called the smartest man in the House.

REGINE: Goes back to your Oxford Union days, no doubt. Finally, a really powerful figure. Power is so sexy as we all know. Even more than money. I've never had either but I can recognise it, particularly in bed.
(*During this, LEONARD and ISOBEL have slipped out. STELLA is questioning WAIN. He nods towards one of the mirrors.*)

WITHERS: Newspapers don't wield power. They *follow* the news just as they *follow* public taste while they pretend they're leading it. They pinch everything, invent nothing, debase everything. We are the hindsight setters. Lovely to see you, Regine. (*He kisses her.*)

REGINE: Oh, Ashley, you've only just arrived. You've barely touched your second drink.

WITHERS: No point in wasting time.

STELLA: I quite agree. (*To SMASH, who is trying to bear hug her out of the room.*) Just a minute, dreamboat. I see that Leonard and Mrs Sands have anticipated everyone.

REGINE: Well, you know what housewives with no job and teenage children are like. And Leonard's quite a dish, in spite of his awful vagueness.

STELLA: Do you mind? (*She moves to one of the mirrors and looks at it.*)

REGINE: Oh, isn't it a bit early for that?

STELLA: Just this one. For a quick flash off of the first action of the evening.

REGINE: Sorry, if you think it dull, darling.

STELLA: I don't. Really. Please. Does anyone mind? (*Everyone looks compliant, mutters of approval. BIGLEY shouts 'Yahoo' and spills his champagne.*)

REGINE: Wain. The mirror. (*WAIN presses a button. They all gather around and stare into the mirror. Pause.*) Good God!

STELLA: They've been in there about forty minutes and they're both sitting on the bed talking like two men in the Athenaeum. Fully clothed.

REGINE: Even got their shoes on. Wain, can we have the sound?

WAIN: Yes, m'lady. (*He presses another switch.*) (*They all listen in silence. Presently LEONARD's voice can be heard loud and clear.*)

LEONARD: (*Voice off.*) Yes. Yes. That's what I felt. Marriage has to be a commitment *and* poetic. But it's like committed poetry. How can you be committed and really, truly poetic? I mean, it's the poetry that matters. Not the rest of the things in isolation. It's the poetry...

ISOBEL: Right. It's that that matters. Then the rest adds up. But if not, no poetry. (*Pause. They all watch and listen intently. Then:*)

LEONARD: (*Voice off.*) You know... do you mind if I talk to you like this?

ISOBEL: No. Anything... please... it's such a relief.

LEONARD: Well – I – I have considerable difficulty – in getting it up...

(*Pause.*)

REGINE: Oh, Christ. Turn it off. It's obscene.

Scene 2

The Bedroom. Furnished as you would expect in this house. ISOBEL and LEONARD are indeed lying fully clothed on the enormous bed, with about four feet between them. They look cheerful and relaxed, pensive but inquiring and obviously enjoying each other's company. Pause.

ISOBEL: Can't you?

LEONARD: What?

ISOBEL: Get it up?

LEONARD: Oh, yes. I didn't say I *couldn't...* I'm sorry I must have confused you. More champagne?

ISOBEL: Please... Thanks.

LEONARD: No, it's not that. Only too facile at times. But other times, well. It's about like lifting a mini by hand. Well, not necessarily hand. You know what I mean?

ISOBEL: Exactly. I shouldn't worry about it. You're wonderfully attractive.

LEONARD: So are you... I knew we'd click the minute I saw you.

ISOBEL: So did I.

LEONARD: Rather conventional, isn't it?

ISOBEL: Very. Do you want me to undress?

LEONARD: Not just yet. Unless you want to. I think *I* might in a minute. This jacket's frightfully hot and that appalling press of people in Regine's sitting room. Did you like it?

ISOBEL: Not much. I couldn't take my eye off you.

LEONARD: Well, I was thinking of you... I got stuck with that awful journalist woman. Asked me insulting questions and then tried to get me to bring her in here for a quick how's-your-father.

ISOBEL: I thought she'd *got* you for a while.

LEONARD: Fortunately, Smash Deel started pawing and fumbling at her and I could get away to you. She's probably with him now. She's listed with him, I dare say.

ISOBEL: You mean Lady Frimley has a *placement* for all this?

LEONARD: Oh, yes. I think we're correctly seated. Just accident though.

ISOBEL: Nice one though.

LEONARD: Very... I say...

(*Pause.*)

ISOBEL: What?

LEONARD: Oh, nothing.

(*Pause.*)

ISOBEL: Wouldn't it be hilarious if we fell in love.

LEONARD: *That's* what I was going to say. But I funked it...

ISOBEL: Did it sound pushy?

LEONARD: No. Courageous. Are you married?

ISOBEL: Yes.

LEONARD: Children?

ISOBEL: Three. You?

LEONARD: Divorced. Three children.

ISOBEL: Snap.

LEONARD: But you're still married.

ISOBEL: For the present...

LEONARD: Isobel... are you religious?

ISOBEL: I don't know. C of E. But I think, I think it frightens me. Much more than sickness or death.

LEONARD: Sick unto death. Oh, yes, you're a religious. I could spot you. That's not to say you're not irreverent with yourself. God is in his invisibility... Yes... Odd place to say it. But *think* about it. What we look for is beyond us. We – are – alone in a room. Two strangers. The Jews had a good idea of the heart. I can see yours moving.

ISOBEL: I know. Feel it.

(*He does. Gently.*)

LEONARD: The Hebrew idea of the heart was – the Whole Man. Not just the intellect. Fools in Christ. We behave

like idiots. That's a bit on the way to heroic... You know
what I said – about not being able to get it up?

ISOBEL: I thought it rather brave... I'm afraid *I'm* not very
good at it.

LEONARD: Aren't you? Neither am I. I don't know...
(*They laugh and pour more champagne. Then*:)
What I have, this thing so despised or ignored – is yours.
It sounds strange. We may never? Or never meet again.
But it *would* be yours, not just *my* object. Yours too.
Ours... Was that too awful?

ISOBEL: No. Not, not awful. Try not to make me tearful,
that's all.

LEONARD: Well, that's something we have in common.
The Gift of Tears. Let's cherish that – and drink to it. (*He
kisses her eyes lightly, then her lips.*) You can never be a
man, you know.

ISOBEL: *You* can never be a woman. Isn't it sublime?

LEONARD: More shampoo? (*He pours.*) For my *REAL
FRIEND*. (*Another light kiss.*) I don't care, you – women
– are the secret of life. *We* are uncertain, undefined,
perhaps unnecessary, as you say... We have to be more:
flamboyant, spurious, enduring, tender, frightened,
over-sensitive and protected, more reckless, indiscreet.
You've been taught that you're a woman of sorts. I that
I'm a man. The Victorians used to, no my father even,
thought manliness was an upright virtue. Like thrift.
Who recommends *thrift!* Nowadays, you can't *consume*
and be thrifty... What was I saying? Girls learn to *be,*
boys to *act.* You are a woman. You are a girl child.
You were a virgin. You became a mother. You *are.* Yet,
like me, us, you are still full of divine discontent.

ISOBEL: I don't think Adam ever *really* lost his rib.

LEONARD: The effort of learning to live as you're
expected to is bad enough. But to find another way
really *is* painful.

ISOBEL: We're none of us sufficiently *prepared.*

LEONARD: Isobel, I think I love you. I do...

ISOBEL: So do I... Is it so strange?

LEONARD: So they'd have us believe. *I* believed it. We've
no – trouble is – we can't have any clear idea of
the future.

ISOBEL: If only it could be an *improved* version of the past.
With its most particular moments. If it could be open but
fixed and discernible.

LEONARD: Pushes white out, drives what in... Have we
gone mad?

ISOBEL: No. Neither one of us. Mistaken perhaps but that's
not madness.

LEONARD: We can never *know* each other. Do you think
you can be unsexed by failure?

ISOBEL: No... more likely success, like those rich young
men in Regine's room.

LEONARD: All-exacting affairs, all-exacting marriages.
No middle ground unless it's just doggerel. You get
pretty sick of doggerel.

ISOBEL: It's the poetry *we're* after.

LEONARD: You're dead right. It's the poetry we're after.
That's the middle bit we're after! Didn't you say that
earlier sometime?

ISOBEL: No. *You* did.

(*LEONARD starts to undress in a rather baffled way, not
yet drunk but slightly confused by his encounter with ISOBEL.*)

LEONARD: Funny, meeting *you* here.

ISOBEL: Yes.

LEONARD: Sorry. Lot. Who said Art is made by the alone
for the alone?

ISOBEL: Don't know. (*She watches him carefully undressing.*)
Sounds true.

LEONARD: Do you? Yes. So do I. That's why we need
Love. Otherwise we *would* be alone. Frighteningly.
There's not that much Art... Doesn't bear thinking
about...

ISOBEL: Don't fret.

LEONARD: Sorry. Dirty habit. In public, anyway.

ISOBEL: I wonder what the others are doing.

LEONARD: Don't care, do you?

ISOBEL: No. I've got – no, she's, Wain's put in some shampoo for real friends.

(*He kisses her. He is now without jacket or trousers. He goes to a concealed built-in fridge and opens another bottle. They toast each other after the silence.*)

LEONARD: To real friends.

ISOBEL: Real friends. Shampoo. Are we being rude to our hostess? Disappearing so soon?

LEONARD: Hell no. That's what we're here for. Well, not us so much. We're more or less nobodies. A whim of Regine's. The whole joint is bugged like Watergate. Two-way mirrors. God knows what.

(*ISOBEL looks slightly alarmed.*)

Don't mind, do you?

ISOBEL: I don't know. They must be pretty busy themselves by this time. Miss Shrift and Smash!

LEONARD: Shall I turn the light off?

ISOBEL: No, please...

LEONARD: You've nothing to worry about. You look heart-bearing.

ISOBEL: Thanks... So do you... (*Looks down at himself.*)

LEONARD: Do I? Really? My wife used to say no man could look sexy in his socks.

ISOBEL: Your wife was wrong.

LEONARD: But right for *her.* But not for you.

ISOBEL: No.

LEONARD: Anyway, if you don't mind, I think I'll take them off. I've got disgusting feet, I'm afraid.

ISOBEL: Go ahead...

LEONARD: I can't believe it.

ISOBEL: What?

LEONARD: About you being no good at it.

ISOBEL: I've been *told.*

LEONARD: Don't believe interested parties – if that's what I mean... Yes, it is.

ISOBEL: I think they were right.

LEONARD: Well, it all – all –

ISOBEL: Yes?

LEONARD: Depends on what – I mean who it is.
  Surely? No?

ISOBEL: Perhaps. But there must be a minimum standard
  of performance.

LEONARD: Yes. Like my not getting it up. Good model but
  difficult to start. Use plenty of choke.

ISOBEL: To at least give pleasure. If not *please*.

LEONARD: You know that's what's nice about women.
  They don't mind your beer belly or your bad breath or –
  bad breath…

ISOBEL: Your grey hair. That's nice.

LEONARD: Ageing.

ISOBEL: You're young. That's what's nice about men.
  They can still be boys and yet men. Women can't do
  that trick.

LEONARD: Not so retarded.

ISOBEL: People think I'm arrogant. They don't know the
  effort it takes… I'm… tired of effort…

LEONARD: My dear. (*Solicitously.*) Take your shoes off…
  (*He takes them off and rubs her feet.*) Better?

ISOBEL: Not bad for a man with your physical
  disadvantages…

LEONARD: My children don't care too much for me.
  What about yours?

ISOBEL: They make excuses for me.

LEONARD: I spent months alone in an Anderson air-raid
  shelter during the war. What with that and school, by the
  time I was sixteen I was heartily sick of myself.

ISOBEL: Life may be hell but who can tell that unknown
  boredom from which no traveller returns.

LEONARD: Perhaps we're reincarnated.
  (*During the rest of the scene, they are both slowly undressing.
  He unzips her at one point. As they chat.*)

ISOBEL: Do you remember *Margaret Rose*?

LEONARD: *Rather*! Have you ever thought of a woman
  er, well: fishing – alone; bird-watching alone; being a
  game-keeper; lighthouse keeper; butterfly collector?
  (*Pause.*)

LEONARD: Don't you worry about your eyesight, Mr Marx? The thing is to use *your* language and not someone else's.

ISOBEL: Exactly. I seem to have been mouthing other people's words all these years... Not my own.

LEONARD: But – well, like in marriage, no, not just marriage: how does one avoid cruelty? And still be honest and *survive*? Do you like nudes? Female, of course. Male doesn't count. It's only fit for photography.

ISOBEL: Yes. I do. It's the eternal subject.

LEONARD: Glorious pursuit of the *impossible*. All nude painting is religious. It's exploring the unknowable.

ISOBEL: Like God.

LEONARD: Distorted bodies, ravaged bodies, sad bodies, proud bodies. All *points* in the great circle... I'm so glad.

ISOBEL: Thanks.

LEONARD: The trouble with my wife was that I *confided* in her. Too much. Too rich for the blood. And it would come back at me later like a brick. No. That was a mistake. Confiding. Overdid it. Not enough restraint. Do you have restraint?

ISOBEL: I ape it. But that's all.

LEONARD: I once knew a couple – both divorced – who married each other because the *children* wanted them to!

ISOBEL: People like that give heterosexuals a bad name.

LEONARD: It's the food of all painters and their nudes, the priests with their clouds of unknowing. Marriage should be a vision of excellence. EXCELLENCE. The stuff they don't make or want any more.

ISOBEL: No demand for it nowadays, madam.

LEONARD: But a *vision*.

ISOBEL: A vision.

(*They turn to look at each other. Pause.*)

LEONARD: I *am* in love with you. (*Puzzled pleasure.*)

ISOBEL: And I with you...

LEONARD: Isn't it extraordinary...?

ISOBEL: Weird...

LEONARD: Shall we?

ISOBEL: Yes…
(*They embrace.*)
LEONARD: Shall I turn the light out?
ISOBEL: No…
LEONARD: Remember –
ISOBEL: Yes?
LEONARD: Well, if I… No, it's going to be all right.
ISOBEL: It will. Desire shall not fail… And you remember…
LEONARD: What?
ISOBEL: It's only a vision.
LEONARD: And that's what we're both after.
ISOBEL: A vision…
(*They embrace.*)

Scene 3

The Sitting Room. Early morning. ISOBEL is lying on a sofa with LEONARD's head in her lap. They are both fully dressed, very sleepy and contented almost to the point of smugness. WAIN comes in with a breakfast tray and sets it down before them. He coughs.

ISOBEL: Oh, thank you, Wain. I'm starving.
LEONARD: So am I.
ISOBEL: After all that exercise. Talk about Olympic Games.
LEONARD: Well, you're certainly the Muhammad Ali of
the century. You *are* the greatest, man.
ISOBEL: And you're the greatest, man.
(*They kiss.*)
LEONARD: Not very good at it! You're the World Cup
winner.
ISOBEL: Can't get it up! Down more likely. *Down*, Fido!
LEONARD: Well, Fido is a bit sore this morning, I
must admit.
ISOBEL: I'm surprised he's still *there*. What about *me*!
My vision's pretty sore round its edges.
LEONARD: Darling. You *are* a vision.
ISOBEL: So are you. Let's eat before we slope off.
(*REGINE enters.*)
REGINE: Oh, good morning, you two. Up already.
Sleep well?

ISOBEL: Not a wink.

LEONARD: Not one.

ISOBEL: Marvellous.

LEONARD: Magnificent.

ISOBEL: Super, comfy bed, Regine.

REGINE: Well, I'm glad it was such a success. You both look as if you've had a – vision.

ISOBEL: We have.

LEONARD: The two of us.

ISOBEL: A flash only –

LEONARD: But such a flash…

ISOBEL: Of the journey.

LEONARD: We don't know where we're going.

ISOBEL: And we never shall.

LEONARD: But we've *started* the journey.

ISOBEL: Together.

LEONARD: Like Paul and Barnabas.

ISOBEL: Perhaps we should re-name ourselves.

LEONARD: You be Paul –

ISOBEL: And you be Barnabas.

LEONARD: Morning, Paul.

ISOBEL: Howdy, Barnabas.

(*They kiss.*)

LEONARD: Had any good visions lately?

ISOBEL: Ecstatic.

LEONARD: So have I.

ISOBEL: But I'm a bit new to this missioning and journeys.

LEONARD: Me too. But we'll pick it up.

ISOBEL: We *have* picked it up.

REGINE: You two are very odd. Don't tell me you've –

ISOBEL: Fallen in love?

LEONARD: Utterly.

REGINE: You *are* mad. Perhaps the country air doesn't agree with you. That champagne was all right, wasn't it, Wain?

WAIN: Yes, m'lady.

REGINE: Have all the others breakfasted?

WAIN: They're all down.

REGINE: Good.

WAIN: Or gone.

REGINE: Gone? Who?

WAIN: The gentlemen, m'lady.

REGINE: But who? Why?

WAIN: Mr Nates and Mr Bigley left in Mr Bigley's helicopter. They said to say: Thanks for all the *wild* entertainment. And they'd 'see you around'. Mr West said he'd not enjoyed himself so much for years. He'd ring you from Fleet Street. He went back to 'file some copy' in his office. Mr Black had to go to a preview in the provinces somewhere. He said to thank you for all the fun and he'd be getting to you about backing his new show. Mr Stewkes apologised but said he had to go to his constituency surgery and also prepare a speech for the House next week about blackmail and vice in the country. Mr Deel's group arrived in a van to take him to a gig in Newcastle. He told me to tell you he'd had a great, funky time. Mr Withers left in his car. He said he had to 'get to the bank as soon as it opened'. He told me to *tell* you. Mr Stan had given him a letter of authorisation.

REGINE: Letter of authorisation! My God, they'll have opened it already.

WAIN: He asked me to give you this note.

(*She tears it open and reads it aloud.*)

REGINE: 'National Newspapers Ltd. Male is gender – chauvinist is excessive love of country. Pigs is ladies' jargon. I know you've been "had" many times but not like this. Thank you for a delightful and enjoyable stay in your gorgeous place. Kindest wishes for now and the future, yours gratefully and patriotically, Ashley Withers.' The snake!!

LEONARD: Not pigs.

ISOBEL: I *like* piggies.

REGINE: Get Mr Stan, will you.

WAIN: He's putting his suitcases in the car, m'lady.

REGINE: Suitcases! Everyone's gone mad! Get him in here.

(*WAIN goes out. STELLA, LETITIA, JOG and GWEN enter.*)

STELLA: *I'm* mad with that Smash Deel. My wrist is falling off. How were yours?

LETITIA: So-so. Usual.

GWEN: Draggy.

JOG: Real PIGGY. Horrible. Men! They won't know what's *hit* them.

STELLA: Those two look very starry.

REGINE: *They're* in love, my dear.

FOUR GIRLS: In love!

STELLA: Is there a doctor in the house!

LETITIA: What larks!

GWEN: But is he filthy rich or something?

JOG: *Just filthy*! Ugh!

REGINE: Everything's gone wrong. There's been a plot to bring us down.

JOG: Counter-revolutionary?

REGINE: You bet your life it's counter-revolutionary. And my Stan, my STAN has been the one under the counter right from the outset.

STELLA: Stan. But he's a, a NO-man.

REGINE: He's a man all right. Treacherous. Betrayer. (*Calls.*) Stan! Stan! Judas!

(*STAN comes in armed with camera equipment and a plane ticket in his hand.*)

STAN: Call me?

REGINE: Where do you think you're going?

STAN: Sunny Spain.

STELLA: On holiday?

STAN: No. To live. For good. Nice and luxurious. Own villa, birds, everything.

REGINE: To *live*! What about *us*?

STAN: You've got this, haven't you? Anyhow, we're not married or anything like that.

REGINE: Where's last night's film and photographs and everything?

STAN: Gave them to the newspaper proprietor geezer. Withers.

REGINE: You *gave* it to him! (*It really is sinking into her now.*)
And the rest! All the archives! The boxes! The bank!

STAN: Oh, he's got the lot.

REGINE: *All* of it!

STAN: All of it. He just rang me to say he'd got it safely.
I'm picking up my cheque on the way to the airport.

REGINE: Cheque!

STAN: How else do you think I can live in Spain for the
rest of my life and never lift a finger?

STELLA: You little *rat!*

LETITIA: Traitor!

GWEN: Scum!

JOG: Fascist!

STAN: Well, I'll be off then. 'Bye, ladies. Nice seeing you.

ISOBEL: Good night, ladies. Sweet ladies...

LEONARD: Good night, good night, good night.

JOG: You won't get away with this! We'll start the fight all
over again. *All* revolutions have their setbacks and traitors.

STELLA: My God. All over again!

REGINE: All that work and preparation. It'll take *years.*

JOG: Don't fail now, comrades! This will make us *stronger,*
not *weaker.*

LEONARD: It's like the Lisbon earthquake. You can
interpret its meaning to suit your own prejudice.

JOG: Shut up, you *beast!*

LEONARD: To rail is the privilege of the loser. Anyway,
men's sins are mostly venial rather than venereal, as *you*
appear to believe.

JOG: We *hate* you, all of you. *Hate* you.

LEONARD: In the case of you ladies, perfect hatred
understandeth all things.

ISOBEL: And perfect hatred casteth out all fear.

STELLA: What are you: a double act?

STAN: Well, I'm off then. Don't try to do anything *I* can.

REGINE: Good riddance!

ALL FOUR: Pig!

STAN: Well, honk honk and tickerty boo! (*He leaves.*)
(*JOG is almost having a fit.*)

Characters

WILFRED

JILL

JERRY

MARY

JACK

MARK

GIRL ON TRAIN

WAITER

WILLIE

GUARD

PORTER

MILLS

CLUB MEMBER

CABBIE

WOMAN ON TRAIN

POLICEMAN

Jill and Jack was first transmitted by Yorkshire Television on 11 September 1974, with the following cast:

WILFRED, Stanley Lebor

JILL, Jill Bennett

JERRY, Denis Lawson

MARY, Wendy Gifford

JACK, John Standing

MARK, Michael Byrne

GIRL ON TRAIN, Alison Mead

WAITER, Alan Bowlas

Director, Mike Newell

Producer, Peter Willes

Scene 1

Exterior. Night.

A discreet but expensive car turns off a busy London street and makes its smooth, chauffeur-driven way into the leafy space of an attractive square. It stops outside one of the tall early nineteenth-century houses. The uniformed chauffeur emerges to open the door for JILL who steps out unhurriedly from reading her paper from the lamp in the roomy comfort of the back. She is attractive and dressed in the most strikingly stylish but succinctly everyday way.

WILFRED: Your brief-case, madam.
> (*He hands it to her and she takes it, folding her paper carefully but naturally.*)

JILL: Thank you, Wilfred. How long do we need to get there?

WILFRED: Oh, twenty minutes should be about right in this traffic.

JILL: Right. I'll be out in fifteen. Just in case there are any hold-ups on the way.

WILFRED: Very good, madam.

JILL: Don't want to keep him waiting. You know how they worry.

WILFRED: That's right, madam.
> (*She goes up the steps to the front door, which is opened by JERRY, a young man in a smart white jacket.*)

JERRY: Good evening, madam.

Scene 2

Interior. Entrance hall. Night.

JILL: Evening, Jerry. Put my brief-case in the study on my desk, will you.

JERRY: Yes, madam.

JILL: Only I may have to go over a few things later – if I get the chance.

JERRY: Your evening papers, madam.

JILL: Thanks.
> (*Takes them.*)
> Only I've got to dash.
> (*Unhurried, she glances at papers.*)

JERRY: Hectic day, madam?

JILL: Just the usual, Jerry. Just the usual. Frantic but fun…
Fun but frantic. I could do with a drink while I'm
changing.
> (*She advances towards the stairs, taking in the headlines and
> stop press.*)

JERRY: I put some of the Chablis on ice in your room.

JILL: Thanks. Miss Kaye in?

JERRY: In her room. I think she's taking someone to
the theatre.

JILL: (*To self.*) That self-loving squirt Robert, I suppose.
> (*She goes upstairs.*)

JERRY: You are *both* dining out tonight?

JILL: Yes. I shall be at my club. But there shouldn't be
anything. So you might as well go out for
the evening.

JERRY: That's very nice, madam. I'll leave everything out
you might need when you come in.

JILL: Thanks.

Scene 3

Interior. Upstairs corridor. Night.

Following JILL, past good paintings, furnishings, etc., into:

Scene 4

Interior. JILL's bedroom. Night.

*It is large, with a double bed and all sorts of dizzy consumer luxuries
like hi-fi, fridges, etc., leading on to her own leafy, exotic bathroom
and dressing-room. A parrot swings in the bathroom, highly coloured,
cheerful, called WILLIE. She turns on some music and starts to
undress methodically and without particular hurry. Clearly, she has*

the operation timed to a second. Still glancing at the headlines and back pages for the racing results, she goes to her large wardrobe.

JILL: Damn.

WILLIE: Damn!

JILL: Evening, Willie. That horse was nowhere. You gave me the wrong tip.

WILLIE: Nowhere! Nowhere! Damn!

JILL: I wish you'd draw me a bath and shut up, you dozy, past-it old pullet.

(She makes a quick selection from an almost endless line of dresses and shoes and places them on the bed carefully.)

Scene 5

Interior. Bathroom. Night.

JILL: Nothing to wear, as usual.

WILLIE: Past-it old pullet.

JILL: *You* are, not me!

(She draws the bath, goes back and pours herself some wine from the waiting bucket. She carefully selects stockings from a drawer as she buzzes the house phone.)

(On phone.) Jerry! I've just tried the wine. It can't be the usual...no, I know it wasn't. Chateau Y-Front sixty-nine I'd say. Send it back, will you. Can't think *what* they're doing. Right...

(As she puts down the receiver, there is a knock on the door.) Mary? Come in.

(MARY enters, dressed for a big evening.)

MARY: Hullo! Rush?

JILL: No. I've six minutes or so. You?

MARY: Well, you know Robert. He'll only fret if I'm not there first.

JILL: How would he *know*?

MARY: He'd just *know*, that's all. Right?

JILL: I *do* know, thanks.

MARY: Shagged?

JILL: Drink'll put me right. That bloody horse didn't come in.

MARY: Not anywhere?

WILLIE: Not anywhere!

JILL: Willie – shut up. I'll cut off your beak at *both* ends.
> (*All very light, by the way. Like the rest, in fact.*)

Where you off to then? Not that bloody Crush Bar again?

MARY: He likes it. Got to keep 'em happy.

JILL: Suppose so.

MARY: And it's Nureyev or something and he likes to be *seen*. Yes. SEEN! You know how they like to be *seen*.

JILL: That's all they go for as far as I can make out.

MARY: And you?

JILL: Just the club.

MARY: Bit dull for him, isn't it?

JILL: He doesn't seem to mind. As long as he's with me.

MARY: Lucky old you.

JILL: There's my bath.

WILLIE: Bath's nowhere!
> (*JILL goes over to the bathroom.*)

MARY: You'll be late.

JILL: *You* will. And you know what *that'll* do to the evening.

MARY: Don't I just! Two ten quid tickets for nowt. See you.

JILL: No oats if you don't *run* for 'em! 'Bye.

MARY: Have fun!

JILL: Oh, I think I shall…
> (*She watches MARY go out. As she turns into the bathroom for her bathing cap, WILLIE shouts past.*)

WILLIE: Have fun! Nowhere! Have fun. Have fun.

Scene 6

Interior. JACK's flat. Night.

In the inner suburbs which he shares with MARK. Perhaps, at this point it should be made absolutely clear that neither JACK nor MARK are remotely 'Gay' to use the fashionable cant word. The same applies to JILL and MARY. They are very much two chaps and two girls. It is merely that their social roles have become rather confused, if not completely reversed. JACK is sweating in front of the mirror trying to fix his bow tie before putting the finishing touches to his evening outfit.

JACK: Oh, great balls of bleeding fire. Why did I have to put on a new shirt. Sackfuls of plastic knicker elastic and pins and cardboard. Damn plastic.

MARK: (*Appears round door.*) And down with elastic. Can I help?

JACK: Why can't I buy a decent shirt! Instead of this floppy dicky's night out!

MARK: Car's here.

JACK: Tell him he can wait.

MARK: Train won't.

JACK: Could you give us a hand?

MARK: Easy as winking. Don't panic. You want to look your best. All that. That's what they want...
(*He helps tie-making.*)

JACK: 'Course it is. Then when we look like a bundle of old rags... Bless you, old boy. You are good at these things.

MARK: Have to be, old darling. Don't we all? There we are!

JACK: May the Good Lord bless you and all that. I could kiss you. In fact I will.
(*He does, perfunctorily.*)
Hand me my jacket, will you?

MARK: *Very* nice! Present?

JACK: Her.

MARK: Thought so. Bang-on taste.

JACK: (*Anxious.*) I say, old boy, you don't think –

MARK: You look –

JACK: The waistcoat's a bit –

MARK: What?

JACK: Well...poncified.

MARK: She'll adore it. And the watch and chain.

JACK: Really?

MARK: Really.

JACK: You're not just saying that. She's so meticulous herself. I'd hate her to think...

MARK: Think?

JACK: Well, that I'm all done up like a dog's dinner just because I want her to, well, you know.

MARK: Rubbish. She'll be thrilled with you. So she should be. Some girls'd go potty. What's that?

JACK: What's what!

MARK: Scent?

JACK: Oh, God – do I smell? I did my armpits. My socks gleaming like confetti. Pure, fresh. *Do* I look an ass?

MARK: No. Irresistible.

JACK: You don't think I should put on the old trusty green and brown –

MARK: Pinstripe. No. I don't.
(*Horn honks outside.*)
Now get your skates on. You know how it irritates them if you're a few minutes late.

JACK: Thanks, dear heart. You've been a brick.
(*He dashes to the door.*)

MARK: Have a nice evening. Relax. She'll adore you.

JACK: Oh, I hope so. Oh, oh, my overnight case.

MARK: Do you think you should?

JACK: Well, we'll see. Depends how she – er – puts it.

MARK: She knows how to behave. Well, I'll see you. Or not.

JACK: Yes. Or not.
(*Horn off.*)

MARK: Go on!

JACK: Yes. Great night. Big deal. I'll never get through it. Oh, my gawd!

Scene 7

Exterior. House. Night.

He stumbles down the steps outside and falls into the waiting cab.

MARK: (*Calling out.*) Bonne chance!

JACK: Thanks, old boy. Bless you.

CABBIE: Well?

JACK: Station!

Scene 8

Exterior. Railway station. Night.

JACK dashes through the barrier, past the ticket inspector and is assisted on to the moving train by a porter.

Scene 9

Interior. Crowded railway carriage. Night.

JACK is looking rather flushed and uneasy, as he stands, clutching his overnight case. A YOUNG GIRL looks up at him curiously from her seat.

YOUNG GIRL: Excuse me, but are you feeling all right?
JACK: Yes, thank you.
YOUNG GIRL: (*Starting to rise.*) You look to me as if you'd be better sitting down.
JACK: No, really, thank you. I think I need a bit of fresh air.
YOUNG GIRL: Very well. If you're sure.
    (*She goes back to reading her paper and he gropes his way through the door to the corridor.*)

Scene 10

Interior. Railway corridor. Night.

JACK stumbles his way past bad-tempered passengers to the lavatory. It is marked 'engaged'. He waits and presently a man and a woman emerge. He turns cheerfully to a man who has to stand back.

JACK: Well, perhaps they *are* engaged! (*He goes in.*)

Scene 11

Interior. Railway train lavatory. Night.

JACK tidies himself up, hair, collar, tie, waistcoat, etc. Presently, a woman's voice is heard as there is a banging on the door.

WOMAN: (*Voice over.*) How much longer are you going to be!

Scene 16

Exterior. Night.

Neoclassical exterior of JILL's club. The car draws up.

JACK: Damn! It's raining.

JILL: Never mind.

JACK: I *do* mind. I only went to the crimpers this afternoon.

JILL: Wilfred's got the umbrella, haven't you, Wilfred?

JACK: Especially. Cost me two quid. It's *pouring*! What about my jacket? Mark pressed it for me particularly.

JILL: It'll be all right.

JACK: I can't do these things myself…all right!

    (*He snorts at the rain and churlishly lets himself be escorted out of the car under the cover of WILFRED's umbrella. JILL follows him, uncovered in the rain. In the entrance to the club, JACK shakes himself like a frenzied dog.*)

JILL: There! Wasn't much. All right?

JACK: (*Glaring.*) What do *you* think?

    (*JILL bites her lip slightly and turns to WILFRED.*)

JILL: Put the car in the corner garage, will you, Wilfred? I'll drive us home.

WILFRED: Very good, madam.

JACK: Are we going to stay out here all night? I'm bloody freezing.

JILL: You and I have got an early start in the morning.

WILFRED: Yes, madam.

JACK: Oh, *do* come on!

JILL: Coming, darling.

WILFRED: Good night, madam.

JILL: Good night, Wilfred. Have a nice evening.

WILFRED: Thank you. Very kind of you. Good night, sir.

JACK: Oh!!

    (*He blunders bearishly through the glass doors, assisted by WILFRED. JILL follows.*)

Scene 17

Interior. Club. Night.

Vast spiral staircase. Like the Reform or Travellers' etc. JILL nods genially to the CLUB PORTER in his glass fortress, who responds with nice respect. JACK is still brushing himself down.

JACK: My shirt looks a right old mess.

JILL: Don't fret. Honestly, darling –

JACK: Would you show me to the Men's – if you've got one in this place.

JILL: Certainly. (*To the PORTER.*) Would you show my guest to the Gentlemen's cloakroom?
(*PORTER nods and leads JACK up the first bank of stairs to the right.*)

JACK: I can't possibly go in like this.

JILL: Take your time, darling. I'll have a drink ready for you.

JACK: Oh – aren't you going to wait for me, then?

JILL: I'll be in the bar. You know how long you take. The porter will show you.

JACK: Oh, all right then.
(*He disappears with the PORTER.*)

Scene 18

Interior. Club. Night.

JILL proceeds on her way up the great staircase. She nods to one or two other lady members. All over the walls are portraits of women in Judges' wigs, academic gowns and so on. Upstairs she settles into a huge leather armchair. A club servant (MILLS) approaches.

MILLS: Good evening, madam.

JILL: Evening, Mills.

MILLS: Usual?

JILL: Please, Mills. For two. Ah!
(*Her face, which has been slightly strained, lightens as a fellow member approaches her.*)

Scene 19

Interior. Club. Night.

JACK enters the room, uneasy in the unfamiliar surroundings and still slightly petulant. The other member drifts off.

JILL: Over here, darling. Drink's all ready.

JACK: (*Sits.*) Oh, there you are.

JILL: Your favourite. All right now?

JACK: Just about.

JILL: That's good then. Cheers.

JACK: Cheers. Sorry to keep you waiting.

JILL: Couldn't matter less. We've all evening.

JACK: Yes. You seemed to be enjoying yourself with your friend. Who's she then?

JILL: Just another member. Nice, lively girl. Very bright.

JACK: I'm sure. Business, I suppose. Talk, talk, talk...

JILL: We don't discuss business here.

JACK: Oh, what do you *discuss* then?

JILL: We come for, oh, the usual, companionship, conviviality. To enjoy ourselves. Which is what we're going to do tonight.

JACK: Yes...

JILL: I've ordered a smashing dinner. Your favourite asparagus and – oh, you'll see.
(*Pause.*)
Drink OK.?

JACK: Fine.

JILL: I think they make the best in London.

JACK: Yes?

JILL: Yes... What do *you* think?

JACK: Wouldn't know.

JILL: Well, cheers, my darling.

JACK: What?

JILL: To us.

JACK: Oh, yes.
(*He raises his glass. Pause.*)

JILL: Comfortable in that chair?

JACK: My shirt's still damp.

JILL: I'm sorry.

JACK: Oh, does it show?

JILL: No. Not at all.

JACK: Where?

JILL: Not anywhere. Really.

(*Pause.*)

JACK: Have I done anything wrong?

JILL: Wrong? Why?

JACK: Oh, I don't know. A bit –

JILL: What?

JACK: Oh, nothing. I'll only put my foot in it.

JILL: A bit what am I?

JACK: Oh – funny, that's all.

JILL: In what way 'funny'?

JACK: Oh, forget it. Maybe it's me as usual.

JILL: You?

JACK: You are pleased to see me, aren't you?

JILL: I've been looking forward to it all day. I couldn't
think of anything else.

JACK: Is everything all right?

JILL: Why shouldn't it be?

JACK: Don't shout at me.

JILL: I'm *not*!

JACK: It's just that I get these funny feelings.

JILL: We're together, that's all that matters.

JACK: Insecure. I know it's a bore to someone like you.

JILL: Darling, you're never a bore to me.

JACK: You mean I am to others.

JILL: Nobody thinks you're a bore. Least of all me.
I adore you…

JACK: Oh, well, sorry.

JILL: Darling…relax… Hungry?

JACK: Gone off it a bit. All that bloody rain. I don't mean
to moan.

JILL: You're not moaning. Anyway, why shouldn't you have
a good old moan? Tell me. I've had quite a day myself.

JACK: Oh, well, of course, it's nothing like you –

JILL: Now, come on –

JACK: Only I did want to see you so much and be at my best.

JILL: Yes?

JACK: And everything seemed to go wrong.

JILL: I know. But that's done with.

JACK: I *suppose* it is.

JILL: Think how lucky we are. There – you look better already!

JACK: Then I *was* looking awful!

JILL: No! Have another? Mills! Two more.

(*Pause.*)

JACK: Not many blokes here.

JILL: Busy time of year.

(*Pause.*)

JILL: *I* had rather a successful week.

JACK: Oh?

JILL: In fact, what you might call triumphant.

JACK: That's nice for you.

JILL: Yes.

(*Pause.*)

Shall we go down? I ordered for eight.

JACK: I haven't had this other drink yet.

JILL: Ah, no.

JACK: I'm sorry I can't swallow these things right down like you can.

JILL: No.

JACK: I'll leave it if you like.

JILL: No, please take your time.

JACK: I didn't know there was a rush on.

JILL: There's no hurry at all. The table will wait.

(*She looks at her watch. Pause.*)

JACK: You did say we had all evening.

JILL: We have, my darling. We have.

(*She smiles at him as he sips his drink very slowly.*)

JACK: Do they have any olives here?

JILL: Sure. Mills!

JACK: Oh, don't bother. I just thought I fancied some.

JILL: Then you shall. Mills!

JACK: I say, you are good.

(He touches her hand, then looks around the room curiously.)

Scene 20

Interior. Club dining room. Night.

JILL and JACK at table. She is talking to the WAITER while JACK looks unconcernedly round the room.

JILL: Ah yes, I forgot. You've decanted the claret.
Then we'll have the sixty-nine now. All right, darling?

JACK: What? Oh, you know me. Don't know one from another.

(JILL nods and the WAITER opens and pours a bottle of champagne, which she approves.)

JILL: Well, then, that's all done.

JACK: What's done?

JILL: Let's talk about you.

JACK: *(Interested.)* Oh, nothing really. I did those two weeks at Watford but I wasn't right for the part, the director hated my guts, none of the London Press bothered to come and the weather kept the customers away to say nothing of the play. I didn't get that modelling job for pipe tobacco which I was depending on to pay for the jacket.

JILL: Won't you let me –

JACK: No, it's smashing of you but you know what I feel about that. So then I had this almighty row with my father about getting a proper job as he calls it and then Leeds went and lost at home two nil...

Scene 21

Exterior. Club entrance. Night.

Rain pouring.

JACK: It's worse if anything.

JILL: At least it's warmer. Now you stay there in the warm. Won't be a minute.

(*She dashes into the rain and disappears down the street while JACK huddles in the warm portals of the club.*)

Scene 22

Exterior. Club. Night.

JILL's car draws up. She gets out, opens an umbrella and rushes over to the club entrance and ushers the waiting JACK into the car. She whips round beside him and starts up the car.

JILL: There! That wasn't so bad.
JACK: Depends on your point of view.
JILL: Now for a nice warming drink.

Scene 23

Interior. JILL's sitting room. Night.

She is standing by the fireplace. He is sitting.

JILL: Another?
JACK: No thanks. I must go in a minute...
JILL: I'm sorry if I upset you.
JACK: You didn't. I'm jolly flattered.
JILL: Please, will you, stay the night? Just as usual.
JACK: I'm sorry, darling. But I don't feel like it tonight. And I seem to be having one of my odd spells at the moment... You see, I... I never expected you to bring up marriage...
JILL: I know. I did rather spring it...
JACK: Do you love me for *myself*? Why should you pay for *me*? My beer money, clothes? You see... Well – marriage.
JILL: I know. It was a mistake. Forget it.
JACK: I can't. You know I love you. But –
JILL: Marriage...
JACK: And it isn't just career and all those things. One can arrange all that if you're intelligent. But, well,

I know I'll never get into the Big League – in anything
– not like you –

JILL: Oh, come.

JACK: As for children. Well, I quite like my nieces and
other people's.

JILL: But looking after them yourself.

JACK: Well, you know what nannies are like. You're at *their*
mercy and it's someone else in the house...babysitting,
growing up, education, all that. And it goes on for so
long. I mean small babies are all right but they do grow
and who knows what. You should see Mark's nephew.
He's *gruesome* and only fourteen. Fourteen years of that.

JILL: We needn't –

JACK: No. I know how you really feel. And some time it
would come up. Bound to.

JILL: I'm sorry...

JACK: So am I... I'd better go –

JILL: I'll take you to the station.

JACK: It's not much of a place. But it's mine and *I* like it...
Mark and I get on pretty well... He has *his* girls and
I – Oh, my darling.

(*They embrace passionately.*)

I expect you've got to get up at dawn.

JILL: More or less.

JACK: At least I can lie in. I'm playing squash in the
afternoon. Let me get a cab. Please.

JILL: No, you won't.

(*She touches his lips. They embrace again.*)

Scene 24

Exterior. Railway station. Night.

*JILL and JACK dash from the car. JACK can't find his ticket. She
buys him one, while he fusses over his overnight case with the ticket
collector at the barrier. She finally gets him on to the leaving train,
kissing him quickly, then watching the train disappear. She slowly
walks back down the platform to her car.*

Scene 25

Interior. JILL's bedroom. Night.

She is changing into a very dashing dressing gown over her night clothes and MARY knocks and enters.

MARY: Hullo. Alone?

JILL: Yes. All alone.

MARY: How'd it work out?

JILL: What they call 'all for the best' I dare say. You?

MARY: Oh. He had to get up early and didn't get any sleep last night – dancing the night away.

JILL: And the evening?

MARY: Nobody noticed him.

WILLIE: Nobody noticed him!

JILL: Shut up, Willie. I've had enough tonight.

MARY: Tell me, if it's not impertinent: how was he in the sack?

JILL: Not much.

MARY: I know. But thought he was great?

JILL: Right.

MARY: Oh, well, back to the address book.

JILL: I can do without, thanks. All for what?

MARY: Maybe you're right. Soldier on a bit, perhaps. 'Night. Sweet dreams.

JILL: 'Night.

MARY: Men…

(*She goes out.*)

WILLIE: Men!

(*JILL picks up her brief-case and opens papers on to her desk.*)

JILL: Who needs 'em.

WILLIE: Who needs 'em!

(*MARY looks in the door.*)

MARY: You won't let Willie chatter on about himself, will you? I've an early start!

(*JILL goes to the bathroom to put cloth over WILLIE's cage.*)

JILL: So have I.

WILLIE: So have I! Men! So have I!

MARY: Do you think it was because he's an actor?

JILL: No. Not at all. He was self-involved, vain; out of touch with everything except his own deficiencies.

MARY: Yes. I suppose so.

JILL: Also –

MARY: What?

JILL: He had NO… INNER… LIFE – that's all.

MARY: Well, you've shut up the bird.

JILL: It's not difficult.

(*MARY goes out. JILL, at her desk, puts on her spectacles and switches on a record. The parrot is quiet in his darkened cage.*)

The End.

INTRODUCTION

A Place Calling Itself Rome

Helen Osborne

A *Place Calling Itself Rome* has never been performed. Re-reading it now, in the present political climate, this doesn't seem so surprising. Like Ridley Scott's *Blade Runner*, there is a threatening, prophetic whiff of mobocracy about it. You only have to be in Leicester Square on a Saturday night to know what I mean.

Coriolanus's political and personal downfall lies in his refusal to cheapen his ideology on the hustings with empty promises to the citizens' demands for surety on 'Wages, prices, rehabilitation, work hours, conditions…' His belief in the intelligence of individualism – elitism, if you like – had no place in the Old Roman/New Labour world of opportunism and calculated rhetoric.

Conversely, his sleek old friend Menenius is an unashamed hector: 'People will save for homes, but where will they be built? But they will be built! Young marrieds, elder citizens of Rome…We expand, the demands grow daily, the claim on resources is immense. Where next, you ask? Rome is the place we make of it!'

Just listen. Close your eyes. Emperor Blair to the very life.

'Oh, world, what slippery terms,' says Coriolanus, undone by betrayal, violence and hatred, his ideals and life crushed and trampled under by the system the citizens have so greedily and blindly embraced.

And yet…Coriolanus: the man who refused to trim. It's a noble epitaph, now as then. But a dangerous one.

Shropshire, 2000

A PLACE CALLING ITSELF ROME

Characters

CAIUS MARCIUS CORIOLANUS

COMINIUS
general against the Volscians

TITUS LARTIUS
general against the Volscians

MENENIUS
friend to Coriolanus

SICINIUS VELUTUS
Tribune

JUNIUS BRUTUS
Tribune

YOUNG MARCIUS
son to Coriolanus

TULLUS AUFIDIUS
general of the Volscians

VIRGILIA
wife to Coriolanus

VOLUMNIA
mother to Coriolanus

VALERIA
friend to Virgilia

ROMAN PARATROOPER

RADIO SIGNALLER

MESSENGERS

POLICE OFFICERS

CITIZENS

SENATORS

MEDICAL ORDERLIES

ROMAN AND VOLSCIAN SOLDIERS

LIEUTENANTS TO AUFIDIUS

MOB

The action takes place in Rome, Corioli and Antium

ACT ONE

Scene 1

Rome. The bedroom of CAIUS MARCIUS. He lies beside his wife VIRGILIA, staring at the first light as it begins to cut more clearly across the bed. He cries out, half waking.

CAIUS MARCIUS: Corioli! Aufidius!

VIRGILIA: What?

CAIUS MARCIUS: Corioli!

VIRGILIA: Um. (*She turns to lie on his neck.*) Sh!

CAIUS MARCIUS: What?

VIRGILIA: Dreaming.

CAIUS MARCIUS: Yes.

VIRGILIA: What time is it?

CAIUS MARCIUS: Early. Go back to sleep.

VIRGILIA: So it is. I will. You woke me with your 'Aufidius' and your 'Corioli'.

CAIUS MARCIUS: I'm sorry.

VIRGILIA: And you?

CAIUS MARCIUS: I will… Virgilia…

VIRGILIA: What is it? It's so early! What's about Corioli? And Aufidius? Where are you going?

CAIUS MARCIUS: Nowhere. Sleep.

(*She turns over and he kisses her.*)

VIRGILIA: You're not to go to old Corioli.

CAIUS MARCIUS: No. You're right. Not for the while. (*He pats her hair and goes to the window.*) Does the light disturb you?

(*She makes no answer but her heavy breathing returns soon.*)

I'll close this bit of curtain…

(*He sits at a table and switches on a tiny light which serves to isolate his wife in more darkness. Taking out a notebook, he writes in an unsure hand.*)

Concentration difficult. More so today. Woke suddenly. Foot almost through the sheet. Today more difficult… sure to. Senate…people…crowds. Tribunes and all of

147

that! No chance of waking *her* again... A few more hours... And years, not years. Surely. Things in flight on first waking... Flying blind. Blind flying. No pilot beside. Just as well... Decisions impossible. But forced ones. Elephants of decisions. Over-weighted. Jostled... Crowds... Hold back... But how? (*To VIRGILIA.*) Am I disturbing you?

(*No answer.*)

Mind racing but no engine. Body concentrates, then flies off. Women. Thoughts of women. All of them. More all the time. Can't write, die to write...*dictate*... Sex flickers, no flame. What to even consider. To do. Coherent? No. Speech even surprisingly blurred. Early. But Senate. Crowds. Hold back. And not just by morning. No, not later...later. Tears far too close, close too hard. At bedside. Rising After Rising Use After Tears! Absurdities, lying *aware*. By the bath. Locked in. One hour. Half. Twenty minutes. Six. Don't. No further. *Don't* get light. No light. Bother? Rightly? Power without storage. Eaten little. Four, no, what, five days. Up. Thrown up. Slime, squalid slime on beard and towels. Mustn't let it be shown. Laundry. *They* know. No. They – don't. Bath. Dread the water. Teeth unclean but nothing will trick *them* up. Mustn't. Bed. Got an hour. No. Fifty minutes... Drank that much. Did I? No. Yes... No. What action? Action? Just spectacle. Bombast... Wrote to my mother. Wrote? I made marks. Perhaps she will die? No. She won't. She's young. Younger than I. That's for certain.

VIRGILIA: Come back to bed.

CAIUS MARCIUS: Coming.

VIRGILIA: Do you want to talk?

CAIUS MARCIUS: No.

VIRGILIA: Eat?

CAIUS MARCIUS: No. But thank you.

VIRGILIA: (*Returning to supine position.*) You must be tired.

CAIUS MARCIUS: Yes.

VIRGILIA: *I* am.

(*He starts getting back to bed, turning off the lamp and so on.*)

CAIUS MARCIUS: You must be. (*Hums.*)

> The working class
> Can kiss my arse.
> And keep the Red
> Rag flying high.

(*He settles into bed.*)

VIRGILIA (*Drowsy.*) Why are you singing?

CAIUS MARCIUS: I'm not. With words is...

VIRGILIA: What?

CAIUS MARCIUS: Words is that they, that is, people, expect them to mean either what they say, don't say, or may say...

VIRGILIA: People?

CAIUS MARCIUS: The people. Goodnight.

VIRGILIA: Good morning... Cuddle...

(*Soon there is the sound only of her breath. CAIUS MARCIUS lies in the darkness, then puts on a gown and goes out, leaving the soft sound and darkness.*)

Scene 2

Rome. A street. Light flashes on, dazzling after first scene. The Roman MOB enters. Also police and some troops, discreetly dressed. Note: mob scenes, demonstrations and so on are obviously up to the director's resources, lack of them, taste, inclination, disinclination or lack of it. However, after the dawn unease of the preceding scene, I would suggest something of the following as a pattern for the similar scenes in the play: a cross-section MOB of students, fixers, pushers, policemen, unidentifiable public, obvious trade unionists, journalists and the odd news camera team, sound men, etc., shrills of police horses, linked arms on all sides; screaming girls, banners of the nineteenth-century sort, banners of the modern kind – 'Caius Marcius: Go Fuck Yourself'; 'We Want A Lay Not Delay'; 'One Quarter Owns Threequarters'; 'No More Trix Just A Fix'; the head of a pig with 'Caius Marcius' inscribed on it; 'Caius Marcius is The Berk – let Him Go And Do The Work –'; Roman troops can be in flak jackets and helmets. Patricians like MPs or high-ranking officers. The Volscians more revolutionary in appearance but still often martial, with berets and insignia, etc. When the Roman MOB enters, it can be chanting for example: AU-FID-IUS.

MOB: AUFIDIUS – AU-FID-IUS – AU-FID-IUS!
> (*Laughter, jeers. A flag is burnt centre stage and waved aloft. Banners wave, stones, marbles thrown. Hand-clapping; cheers. A pop group possibly joins in for a while. The chaos and noise is eventually brought under the partial control of the FIRST CITIZEN.*)

FIRST CITIZEN: Hear me! Will you listen to me!

MOB: Go on then. (*Etc.*)

FIRST CITIZEN: We are all, all of us resolved, determined –

VOICE: Get on with it!

FIRST CITIZEN: To die, yes, if we have to, rather than put up with this state of things.

VOICE: What state of things?

FIRST CITIZEN: What state of things he says!

VOICE: Caius Marcius!
> (*Roar.*)

FIRST CITIZEN: Is that not 'state of things' enough for you?

VOICE: More than enough, if you ask me!

MOB: CAIUS MARCIUS OUT! MARCIUS OUT! OUT! OUT! MARCIUS OUT!

FIRST CITIZEN: Then what's the answer!

VOICE: We know the answer all right.

FIRST CITIZEN: Haven't we got teeth then?

VOICE: Yours look as if you'd got 'em for nothing!
> (*Laughter.*)

FIRST CITIZEN: Then let's *use* 'em!

MOB: Use 'em!

SECOND CITIZEN: A word, my good friends!

VOICE: A word, he says. We've had enough bleeding words!
> (*Cheers.*)

FIRST CITIZEN: Don't 'good friends' us – my good friends! The patricians call you 'my good friend' every day. And why? Because they can afford to!
> (*Applause.*)

We aren't their 'good friends'. *We're* too expensive! Are

you still taken in by this patronage and soft sell and big
dealing for other people? Yes, *others*. And what others?
People who were best off dead and long ago. I know this,
you know this, and we know it, and because it's there to
be seen, seen in us, in us, and not some daft, obsolete,
self-perpetuating senate.

(*Roar.*)

SECOND CITIZEN: Tell me. No, let me say something a
moment.

VOICE: Give a chance!

SECOND CITIZEN: Why do you single out Caius
Marcius? Why? Why pick on him?

FIRST CITIZEN: Single out! Do you hear that! *Pick* on
Caius *Marcius*!

(*Shouts.*)

SECOND CITIZEN: Well, why?

FIRST CITIZEN: Because he *is*: is a pig.

(*Roar.*)

And of all pigs, the piggiest of 'em all.

(*Louder roar.*)

SECOND CITIZEN: So *you* say.

VOICE: So say all of *us*!

(*Cheers etc.*)

SECOND CITIZEN: Don't you think he's done something,
cared something –

FIRST CITIZEN: For him*self*.

SECOND CITIZEN: His country.

VOICE: Somebody *do* him. (*Etc.*)

FIRST CITIZEN: That's all past.

SECOND CITIZEN: What is! Past.

FIRST CITIZEN: What I said: everything.

VOICE: You heard: all!

SECOND CITIZEN: All!

MOB: All. (*Etc.*)

SECOND CITIZEN: Isn't there any memory left! Just
malice?

MOB: Get out of it, get stuffed. (*Etc.*)

VOICE: And *you.*

MENENIUS: We *are* you!

FIRST CITIZEN: Come off it!

MENENIUS: I will not come off it. As I've always done.
(*Some cheers.*)
We are for *you*, we are *yours*, you can rid yourselves of us,
whenever you wish! When*ever*. But what then?

FIRST CITIZEN: Then we'll see!
(*Cheers.*)

MENENIUS: But what? We Romans have a surplus of
emotion all right. But what else? Do we have a surplus
of *trade*?

VOICE: When did *I* work last then?

MENENIUS: Right, my good friend. But do you think no
one cares for you? Why do you only bait and assault the
ones who care the most for you?

FIRST CITIZEN: What care did you ever have for us!

MENENIUS: Think of our efforts!

FIRST CITIZEN: I'd rather not.

VOICE: More shooting and 'tighten your belts' and a bit off
the taxes.

FIRST CITIZEN: If you're lucky.

VOICE: Fine fucking *effort*!
(*Roar.*)

FIRST CITIZEN: I've heard enough.

MENENIUS: Rome must be a city worth saving *for*. Not in
the next month. But the years to come.

VOICE: What about the meantime!

MENENIUS: It will be as *mean* and ready as you choose to
make it.

FIRST CITIZEN: Easy laugh!

MENENIUS: We must have faith, confidence.

VOICE: *You're* all right, mate. What about today?

MENENIUS: And *I* say, what of tomorrow? Be patient –

FIRST CITIZEN: While you spout?

MENENIUS: And what else do *you* do, my good friend.

VOICE: Yes, What does *he* do!
(*Roar.*)

MENENIUS: Very well then. We are on the threshold of a
new experience. Let's embrace it, it and a Rome worth
working for. When you talk of revolution so easily, so do
I, so do *I*. I see the revolution of rising expectations.
That – that is what concerns the Senate, your Senate. For
what else is it? We must reconcile all expectations and
try to disappoint none. We may fail in some but we will
succeed in some. A note of steady expansion. We'll not
flinch. No, not from that. But there must be decision-
making too. We must be a true *community*. For us in the
Senate there is a special challenge. Not simply of
book-making, of *priorities*. Major *policies*. Policies.
Policies!
(*His voice is drowned in the chorus of 'Policies'.*)
There may be new methods, new machinery of
government. Some untested, not even installed. As
I told you we Romans have a surplus of *emotion*. What
do the others have? A surplus of *trade*!
(*Cheers.*)
Different hopes to reconcile. People will save for
homes, but where shall they be built? But they will be
built. They will save for journeys to strange places and
time to enjoy. Young marrieds, elder citizens of
Rome, *everyone*.
(*Cheers.*)
We expand, the demands grow daily, the claim on
resources is immense. Where next, you ask? Rome is the
place we *make* of it. No more or less. But it's no place
now for the belly-aching and fouling-up process of
by-passing dogs – as they must be passed by.
We believe, we have to, in ourselves, our children, our
Senate, with all its faults, *our* faults, *our* future. Our
policies! Our *Rome*! The rest will follow!
(*He stands down to an ovation – more or less – from the
MOB. Stands waving and smiling at them. Enter CAIUS
MARCIUS with escort.*)
Welcome. Welcome to you, Caius Marcius.
VOICE: Welcome. Oh, yes, welcome, *Caius Marcius*!

(*Enter SICINIUS VELUTUS, JUNIUS BRUTUS,
COMINIUS, TITUS LARTIUS with other SENATORS.
SICINIUS is a pale-skinned coloured woman.*)
Ah, Sicinius – a late entrance?

FIRST SENATOR: Don't waste your spleen on Sicinius.
The truth is we are really and indeed at war with the
Volscians now.

CORIOLANUS: Fancy. And what will Sicinius do about it?
March for them I've no doubt. But I tell you, they have a
leader already, Tullus Aufidius –

MOB: AU-FI-DI-US.

CORIOLANUS: Who might surprise you all. If I were not
myself, if I am even that, I would like nothing more than
to be Aufidius.

COMINIUS: You have fought –

CORIOLANUS: And will again, by the look of it.

FIRST SENATOR: Then go with Cominius.

COMINIUS: You *did* pledge yourself –

CORIOLANUS: And why shouldn't I keep it? Titus
Lartius, do you think you won't see me go in against
Aufidius? What is it? Pressures is it? 'Comment' is it?
Is it? What is the 'is'?

LARTIUS: No, no 'is', Caius Marcius. I have made my
position clear, I think.

CORIOLANUS: Well done!

MENENIUS: Yes, well said.

FIRST SENATOR: Let's go to the Capitol, most of 'em are
behind us.

LARTIUS: (*To COMINIUS.*) Let's go. (*To CORIOLANUS.*)
Give your support to Cominius. To us you are something
more than an elected deputy.

CORIOLANUS: What deputy ever became leader?

COMINIUS: Dear Marcius, your place is assured and your
recognition *will* come.
(*He raises his hand.*)

FIRST SENATOR: (*To Roman CITIZENS.*) Get off home, to
your families, your workbenches, both sides of industries,
your floors, we shall all sit down.

CORIOLANUS: And get piles or paunches or the both. You've done well today; led from behind and observed from the front. Get the feel of them.

(*He, the SENATORS and the MOB leave in an uproar of banner waving, shouting, singing, journalists weaving, cameras wobbling, some waving to the audience they are performing to. Leaving the two tribunes alone.*)

SICINIUS: Was there anyone ever as arrogant or obvious as Marcius?

BRUTUS: No one.

SICINIUS: When we were chosen as tribunes for the people –

BRUTUS: Did you see his expression?

SICINIUS: See it! Hear it!

BRUTUS: Don't be deceived. When he's moved, which is too much of the time, he will go for anything or anyone, and someone will always be there to listen to him.

SICINIUS: Or record it. But there's a coldness.

BRUTUS: That's right. That's his strength.

SICINIUS: He'll be eaten soon enough. He's got too much conceit in him as it is. Can you see him being bum boy to Cominius?

BRUTUS: Cominius is a decrepit bully boy general grown old. He'll be blamed for being too old, if there's any blame. And if there's any triumph going, Marcius will have the edge on him.

SICINIUS: Besides, Caius Marcius might lose, but, in these days of fashion and upstarts, Caius Marcius is the man to watch.

BRUTUS: He'll be watched all right. Let's go.

SICINIUS: Let's.

Scene 3

Corioli. The Senate House. Enter TULLUS AUFIDIUS with SENATORS.

FIRST SENATOR: So, Aufidius, think Rome knows every which way what's going on here?

AUFIDIUS: Don't you? Everything here or, indeed, anywhere, is known almost before it's happened. I first heard – I think I've got the letter here. Yes. Here it is. They've troopments at the ready. Cominius; Marcius, *your* old enemy. They hate in Rome as much as here if not more so. Titus Lartius, thought a 'good sort'. These three: not bad leaders. Think on it.

FIRST SENATOR: Our army's ready. We never doubted Rome would ever be any different.

AUFIDIUS: We could have taken every town before Rome had woken up to it.

SECOND SENATOR: Bring your army up, Aufidius; but, knowing them. I think you'll find they're still not ready for us.

AUFIDIUS: Not ready? Oh, I'm only talking of certainties and one of those if ever there was one is Caius Marcius. If he and I could just ever *meet* – neither of us can do any more – till that time.

Scene 4

Rome. A room in CORIOLANUS's house. VOLUMNIA, his mother and VIRGILIA, his wife.

VOLUMNIA: What a glum mood you're in. If I had my son for a husband I should hope I'd put a better face on it than you are; considering what he's at. I remember when he was very tiny, he seemed the only thing life would ever yield up to me; I wouldn't let him a wink out of sight. Even so, I don't think I ever held him back the once; always *forward* – at least that's what I tried to do, and now it's no more different than all those other times; oh, long before he became what he is since. Didn't I let him go to a violent, rotten and filthy war? And didn't he come back practically weighed down with citations and awards like he did when he was a schoolboy? I tell you, Virgilia, I am more proud at this moment, if it's possible, than the first time I set eyes on him.

VIRGILIA: Supposing he had fallen back – even a little? Let alone died in all this thrusting and ambition?

VOLUMNIA: 'Thrusting and ambition' you call it! Its very existence was reputation enough for me. If I had a dozen sons and I loved every one of them as much as my – and your – Marcius, I'd rather the whole lot of them snuffed out and for a good cause than one of them come up to Marcius's scratch.

(*Enter SERVANT.*)

SERVANT: Madam, Lady Valeria is here.

VIRGILIA: Forgive me but I'll go.

VOLUMNIA: Indeed you won't. Oh, I see, your husband's gesture; his voice in the air; seeing what he'll *do* to someone like Aufidius. Do you really think he has a chance against such a man, a *man*, a man like ours? I can hear him say 'Come on, you lot. You were all begotten in timidity even if you'd been born in Rome. There's no blood in you. Red piss.'

VIRGILIA: Red piss, as you call it,'s bad enough to watch without more blood.

VOLUMNIA: You cowish little idiot. What do you know about blood?

(*To SERVANT.*) Well, don't keep Lady Valeria waiting.

(*To VIRGILIA.*) We've got lots to chat about.

VIRGILIA: All I can say is, or think is, God save my husband from Aufidius, or indeed anyone like him.

VOLUMNIA: Aufidius! He'd beat him into the ground.

(*Enter VALERIA.*)

VALERIA: Well, hallo.

VOLUMNIA: My dear Valeria.

VIRGILIA: How nice to see you.

VALERIA: But how are you both? Aren't these terrible times? I mean they're just terrible. What are you doing there decorating? But it looks perfectly splendid. And how's the little son, the little grandchild?

VIRGILIA: He's well enough for his age. Thanks to his grandmother's looking after.

VOLUMNIA: I know my grandson. He'd rather be up and about and doing things. One day. Changing things. Worthwhile things. Than moping about the state of things at home.

VALERIA: His father's son all right. And so pretty as well. Do you know, I looked at him last Wednesday for a whole half an hour – that face, that *determination*, what do you call it, resolve. I saw him chase a butterfly in your garden here, and do you know, he wouldn't even let *that* little creature baulk him! I don't know whether it was his falling down and knees all scratched and bruised, but he was in such a rage, that child, in such a *torrent*, nothing could have saved that doomed insect.

VOLUMNIA: Just like his father.

VALERIA: Wouldn't give an inch.

VIRGILIA: Not an inch.

VALERIA: Come along. Let's have some fun together in your lovely garden.

VIRGILIA: I'm not going out of doors.

VALERIA: Not going out of doors?

VOLUMNIA: Oh, she will, you see.

VIRGILIA: No, if you'll forgive me, I won't. I'm not moving from this house; not even into that garden until His Lordship's come back from all his rhetoricising and legalised brawlings.

VALERIA: Come, you mustn't upset yourself. There's lots to do while he's away.

VIRGILIA: It's not that I'm lazy, as you think, or busy as *I* think.

VALERIA: Can't waste time; especially now.

VIRGILIA: I'd rather it used *me* rather than busy my *self*.

VALERIA: Honestly, go along with me because I really do have the most exciting news for you; yes, your husband.

VIRGILIA: There can't be any yet.

VALERIA: No, honestly, I tell you. I heard it last night.

VIRGILIA: What did you hear then?

VALERIA: Well, aren't I telling you? I heard it from a Senator. Simply this: the Volscians have raised an enormous army. General Cominius has taken some battalions or whatever they're called from the Roman Army and, guess who's immediately behind it, but Titus Lartius and your very own husband. By this time they must be fanned out; is that what they call it? Anyway, entrenched or something, in strategic positions or something, right in front of Corioli itself. And from all accounts, they don't mean to stay *there* long. They'll deal with them soon enough, you can take it from me. It's true, I promise you. So come along, you should be pleased.

VIRGILIA: Forgive me, Valeria, I've not yet taken this in.

VOLUMNIA: Oh, leave her alone, Valeria, whatever news you tell her she'll do nothing but mope and be a misery.

VALERIA: I'm beginning to think you're right. Well, see you later. Oh, come along, Virgilia, give yourself a face-lift and forget the war for an afternoon. The dreariness of the winter and strikes and dark evenings.

VIRGILIA: In a word, no. I will not and I must not, so both go and enjoy yourselves.

VALERIA: Please yourself – of course.

(*VOLUMNIA and VALERIA leave VIRGILIA to herself.*)

Scene 5

A bleak, battle-torn area on the outskirts of Corioli. Enter SOLDIERS with CORIOLANUS and LARTIUS. Flak jackets, berets, helmets, rifles, shields, home-made bombs and bottles hurling, the sound of gunfire and sniping, etc. From the flies a parachute descends bearing a heavily armed PARATROOPER. Before this, CORIOLANUS has been observing his descent keenly through binoculars.

CORIOLANUS (*To LARTIUS.*) A fiver they've made contact.

LARTIUS: Ten.

CORIOLANUS: Done.

LARTIUS: Right.

(*The PARATROOPER lands with a clang of boots and rubble and is helped out of his parachute. He approaches CORIOLANUS and salutes smartly.*)

CORIOLANUS: Well, have they made contact?

PARATROOPER: They're giving each other's eyeballs a good going over, sir, but no action as such yet.

LARTIUS: Well, that's a tenner up your spout.

CORIOLANUS: How far away?

PARATROOPER: Mile and a half.

CORIOLANUS: Right, this'll be it soon enough. With
God's good luck, we should blow the bleeding bejesus
out of them in five minutes and back up those poor sods
being shot at out there for damn all. What do you say,
Lartius?

LARTIUS: Let's get to it.

(*The Roman SOLDIERS prepare to advance in splendid
regimental style, poised on the edge of streets, and so on,
when two SOLDIERS of Corioli appear in paramilitary
uniform and nonchalantly waving white flags.*)

CORIOLANUS: So, there you are. Tell me, Tullus
Aufidius, is he still stuck behind your barricades?

FIRST SOLDIER: No, and there's not one of us that's less
afraid of you than he is.

CORIOLANUS: What a strange race they are. All verbal
quirks and long top lips.

(*Sound of drums and sniping.*)

FIRST SOLDIER: D'ye hear that then? That's our lads
alright. We'll rip down our barricades rather than see you
pound us up like dogs but we'll do it when it suits us.
(*More noise of rifle fire off stage.*)
D'ye hear that then? How far away d'ye think that is?
And who do you think it is? That's Aufidius, that is.
D'ye hear what he's doing to your poor under-paid
professionals?

LARTIUS: Get back before someone kills you. Right, lads.
(*The two SOLDIERS retreat, jeering and throwing stones as
the Roman SOLDIERS prepare to stand ground.*)

CORIOLANUS: They don't look afraid, but if they don't,
it's because of no imagination; and without imagination,
take it from me, you won't find much skill, just random
wind. You know your equipment, you know how to use it
and to use it well; and to use your brains, which is a
damn sight more useful than anything they've got to
pitch against us, or ever shall have. Let's get in there,
Titus – why do we let them waste our time with chat and

drums and banners. Anyone who holds back, he'll deal with me and forget he ever heard the word 'regulations'. (*The ROMANS charge down the street with a terrifying noise. For a while, all we hear is the sound of automatic rifles, shouting and so on. After some of this, they are beaten back to behind their coils of barbed wire, armoured vehicles, etc., led by CORIOLANUS.*)

CORIOLANUS: Call yourselves bloody Romans! May the world's pox rot your bollocks off. Let you all stew in the pus of your sisters' cunts so you stink a mile off. You little gooseygander men, what are you *doing*, running from red bog faced layabouts that my six-year-old'd stand up to. Balls of fire! What is this – a whole company without a mark except those shot up the arse! Now hear me! Get those miserable faces turned round the right way and get stuck into it or as sure as God made little apples, and you rotten lot, I'll turn round and I'll start my own private war with you – and make no mistake who'd win. Come on then! Get your fingers out and-we'll-be-in-crumpet-before-them!

(*A gap appears in the barricade at the other end of the street.*) There's an opening! Get in there! And if it isn't your birthday, you weren't *born*.

(*CORIOLANUS dashes through the opening and disappears.*)

FIRST SOLDIER: It's not my birthday.

SECOND SOLDIER: Mine neither. Haven't been born long enough, anyway.

FIRST SOLDIER: Look, they've really got him in this time.

(*Noise and gunfire off from the direction of the closed barricade.*)

SECOND SOLDIER: Short and curly's department this time, I'll bet.

(*Enter LARTIUS.*)

LARTIUS: Where's your commander?

FIRST SOLDIER: Halted at the barricades looks like, sir. Right behind them he was before you could say how's your father. Next thing he's disappeared. All on his tod. Dressed up and nowhere else to go but in.

LARTIUS: Oh, Marcius, only you. No one else.

FIRST SOLDIER: Dead right, sir.

SECOND SOLDIER: Looks like that's it, then.

FIRST SOLDIER: Look, sir.

(*Enter CORIOLANUS, having forced himself back through the barricade obviously seriously wounded and covered in blood. He beckons wildly to LARTIUS.*)

LARTIUS: Well, don't gape at the poor bastard – follow up!

(*A slight pause and the ROMANS follow LARTIUS and bearing CORIOLANUS with them, disappear behind the barricades.*)

Scene 6

Inside Corioli.

Enter two Roman SOLDIERS under fire and stone throwing.

FIRST SOLDIER: Don't fancy that lot.

SECOND SOLDIER: As Caius Marcius says, they're not a lovable lot.

FIRST SOLDIER: I don't want love, I just want out of this ugly bleeding army. Watch it.

(*They duck from a sniper's volley. CORIOLANUS and LARTIUS enter. The first contemplates LARTIUS, very much on his guard.*)

CORIOLANUS: There's a certain sound about ammunition wasting itself. The ill-trained warlike wanker. How do you think our lads have made out?

LARTIUS: On the whole, they've held. As you well know, Caius, if they make mistakes their orders sometimes actually require it. Allowance has to be made for the situations of war, call it what you like. We can't guarantee or legislate against painful or hasty headed decisions, any more than wisdom as well as bravery and initiative.

CORIOLANUS: Aufidius is the man. If we can get *him*! Titus, take what you think you need to mop up the city. What's left I'll take with me to back up Cominius.

LARTIUS: You're wounded. Orderly!

CORIOLANUS: I'm not even wound up yet. A bit of blood letting's good for the likes of me so long as it doesn't

weaken the natural spleen too much when I catch up
with friend Aufidius. Just so long as he recognises me.

LARTIUS: He will!

(*Exit CORIOLANUS.*)

(*To RADIO SIGNALLER.*) Get all officers you can contact
and we'll meet in the old market. If it's still there. Get on
with it.

(*He rushes off.*

*The SIGNALLER disappears into his armoured vehicle. Enter
COMINIUS, looking grim, with SOLDIERS in support.*)

COMINIUS: Take a breather, lads. You did well; like
people'll have learned to expect from Roman troops in
spite of what they say. Sensible and restrained under fire;
and calm and disciplined in retreat. Rest while you get
the chance. They won't leave us for long.

(*The SIGNALLER puts his head out of the radio van.*)

Well? Got anything?

SIGNALLER: Seems like Lartius and Marcius got caught in
a frontal assault from half Corioli. There's a running
battle. But I think Marcius is trying to limit the area.

COMINIUS: Keep contact.

(*Enter CORIOLANUS.*)

CORIOLANUS: Am I too late?

COMINIUS: Not while you are here.

CORIOLANUS: Old devil!

(*They clasp hands.*)

COMINIUS: As usual. Giving them shit where it's needed,
which is everywhere, then belting on. And the men?

CORIOLANUS: All right without their tribunes to make
them down warfare for shorter hours, thank you. They're
well paid to be shot at. If you can be well *paid*. It's
difficult to know which side the fire came from. But why
are you back here?

COMINIUS: We weren't doing so well. I think I followed
the what-ye-call-it battle concept as we went over it.

CORIOLANUS: Move, move, move! Yes... The orders
were Where do they seem concentrated? With
Aufidius?

COMINIUS: Who else?

CORIOLANUS: Let me go back.

COMINIUS: You're in no proper state. Still, I can't say no. Take what you need with you.

CORIOLANUS: Volunteers. And volunteers I *do* mean. The rest can stay behind, those who come for the uniform, the ride, and all the rest of it.

(*They all yell enthusiastically.*)

Well done! But for Aufidius, we need not just the best but the fastest. The rest had better stay here with Cominius.

COMINIUS: Do as he says. Take your pick.

CORIOLANUS: You, you, you, you… (*Etc.*)

COMINIUS: Let's go.

(*They divide and disappear. Enter LARTIUS with Roman TROOPS.*)

LARTIUS: Keep these barricades. If we abandon the outskirts, we'll get holed up inside.

SOLDIER: Yes, sir.

LARTIUS: Watch and try to make contact. Come on.

(*Goes with the rest. Quiet. Then CORIOLANUS and AUFIDIUS are seen to be stalking each other with rifles and/or pistols through street windows and doors and crouching behind rubble and oil cans.*)

CORIOLANUS: (*Shouts.*) I'll have you, Aufidius. You're the one.

AUFIDIUS: And you're mine.

CORIOLANUS: Let's have you.

AUFIDIUS: Let's see you run.

CORIOLANUS: I? RUN! You'd better do better than you're doing now.

AUFIDIUS: Got you.

(*Rapid exchange of fire between them, desperate running and dodging as each almost kills the other. Some VOLSCIANS come to their leader's aid.*)

CORIOLANUS: Reinforcements crawling up, eh, you slum rat! Vermin always need other vermin! See you.

(*He disappears under a volley of fire from AUFIDIUS, who curses to his followers, then also disappears. After a while a*) *badly wounded CORIOLANUS is led in by COMINIUS and troops.*)

COMINIUS: Thank God for you, Caius.

(*Enter LARTIUS.*)

LARTIUS: Have you seen!

CORIOLANUS: Berserk. We've done what we could.

COMINIUS: Rome will know about it and judge for themselves. They always do. And they shall know the truth of it, not some seeking, rabbling accounts of it from outsiders.

CORIOLANUS: (*In pain.*) Ah.

(*Two ORDERLIES attend on him. There are a few cheers.*)
Wait for the reports, the courts, the writers after the events; the ones who'll call *us* bloody and never mind your wounds or skill or patience. They won't tell you then your Roman's better than any other in the world, spat at, abused, cheerful and always shot at. And in their favourite target – the back.

COMINIUS: Be thankful for small tributes. But they won't be small; we'll see to that. Rome shall know.

ALL: Lord Coriolanus!

COMINIUS: Aye, and no joke either. Caius Marcius; Lord Coriolanus.

ALL: Caius Marcius, CORIOLANUS!

(*Cheers.*)

COMINIUS: Rome shall know. I promise you. Titus, set up your headquarters.

CORIOLANUS: Can I just do one thing. An old woman in the street down there – and then I saw Aufidius.

COMINIUS: We'll see to it. Which house?

CORIOLANUS: Ye Gods, I've forgotten! I'm tired suddenly. Is there a drink?

COMINIUS: Let's go in there. That looks nasty. Sergeant!

(*ORDERLIES bear off CORIOLANUS. The rest follow.*)

Scene 7

The camp of the VOLSCIANS. An old hall with trestle tables, maps, flags, guns, bombs, ammunition. Enter AUFIDIUS, bloodstained, with followers.

AUFIDIUS: Well, the town's taken.
FIRST LIEUTENANT: We'll get it back on the right terms.
AUFIDIUS: Terms. I wish I were a Roman at this moment
  – almost. Terms! What terms can be right that *we* don't
  make. Five times I've fought against you, Marcius, and
  always I'm made a meal of. God, if we ever meet again,
  it's his eyeballs or mine. I'll have him all to myself the
  next time.
FIRST LIEUTENANT: He's the devil all right.
AUFIDIUS: Just as bold if not quite so subtle. Nothing, not
  sleep, food, religion, esteem, Capitol; nor all the interests
  of intercedence or arbitration come between me and my
  Marcius. If I find him, in bed with his wife or tied to his
  child and mother, I'll have that heart out and any going
  with it... Go into the city. Find out what's happening,
  hostages, help from outside, any report you can get, any
  source.
FIRST LIEUTENANT: Won't you come?
AUFIDIUS: They're waiting for me at our arranged point
  across the border. Get to it and find out so that I can get
  on accordingly.
FIRST LIEUTENANT: Sir!
  (*Salutes stiffly and goes out, leaving AUFIDIUS brooding in
  the dust and darkness of his trestle table and blackboards.*)

Scene 8

*Rome. A conference room. Informal. MENENIUS is talking
conversationally with TRIBUNES of the people, SICINIUS and
BRUTUS.*

MENENIUS: Well, the indications are, gentlemen, that
  there will be news before the night is out.

BRUTUS: Good or bad?

MENENIUS: If I am informed correctly, not what your
   so-called man in the street will welcome very much;
   knowing as we do how they feel about Marcius.

SICINIUS: Simplest of animals, lambs, to know at once
   who likes you or not.

MENENIUS: Tell me then, who would you say the
   wolf loves?

SICINIUS: The lamb.

MENENIUS: Yes, to destroy him. After using him. Like
   the Plebians would do to Marcius given the merest
   chance.

BRUTUS: He's a lamb all right. Unfortunately he makes
   noises more like a bear.

MENENIUS: He may make the noises of a bear to you and
   me but within the fugitive place that strange sound
   comes from I assure you, gentlemen, there is quite the
   smallest of lambs. Tell me one thing. You are both up
   with the times and know all that's going on. Tell me
   something that seems to escape me at the moment.

SICINIUS: Well?

MENENIUS: What fault do you think that it is, that
   Marcius has that you two may not have even more of?

BRUTUS: I can't think of any he hasn't inherited – like
   most of his kind; and looked after well and brought to
   every dividend you can think of.

SICINIUS: Pride's gilt-edged.

BRUTUS: Some modest trading in old-fashioned Roman
   boasting is always good for a bit.

MENENIUS: How very interesting. Having said that, what
   would you say was the opinion of you here in the city –
   I mean all those of us you'd call 'the other side'? Do you
   know or does it never bother you, I suppose.

SICINIUS: So what is *their* opinion?

MENENIUS: Only that – you understand we are talking of
   pride now – so you won't be angry.

SICINIUS: Why should we?

MENENIUS: Why should you? I can think of very little
   that could ever make you climb down or change your

sides, but as we are just together, the three of us, tell me
what it is you really think; and it'll go no further. Now:
you blame Marcius for the sin of pride.

BRUTUS: We are not exactly alone in that.

MENENIUS: Oh, I know you would not feel it if you were
in any way alone. You have too much on your side,
perhaps the course of history itself. Otherwise you might
appear some time to be no more than just ingenuous
eccentrics or something of the kind. Your talents are too
blessedly childlike to be used anywhere but inside oh,
what; playgroups and working crowds. You talk of pride;
if you could only just once, the once, look inwards and
make a good old inner survey of your own good selves;
see what lies among the old props holding up the faces
of those worked-on seams; that I would like to see
very much.

SICINIUS: Would you, and what *then*?

MENENIUS: I think that you might discover a pair of the
most unmeriting, proud, over-exposed, vicious and
violent middle men and (*To SICINIUS.*) sorry – women,
we have ever had or known in Rome.

SICINIUS: Menenius, let me tell you, let me tell you and
you surely must know it, that everyone knows well
enough what you are and have done for a long time.

MENENIUS: Indeed I do. I have a reputation for wit and
every irony which as we all know, is always disastrous
for a politician. Also that I like good food and wine and
don't prefer the muck in the market place without
questioning, merely because it is the most known and the
most available. On the other hand, when I do believe in
what I say, my malice is wasted as much as anyone
else's. No one believes in that either. If I sit down with
two statesmen like yourself I cannot take you seriously
any more than you me. When you give me your beer or
tea to drink, it just isn't in me to pretend I like the stuff.

SICINIUS: Which is why you love Marcius?

MENENIUS: Which is *one* reason why I love Caius
Marcius. I can't say that you impress me either with your

arguments or the delivery of them; I have to appear to go along with those who say that you are serious and clever. I can only say that I don't like the look of either of you. Even I am a better sight to look on than either of you two; but I am sure you would be the first to agree that this is very inconsequential. Tell me what it is that you see in me; what is it that's so bad; so calculating, so insignificant; so resolutely turned against Rome's future; and only of benefit to my own ends?

BRUTUS: Come, sir, we know you.

MENENIUS You don't know me, yourselves, or any other damn thing. Oh, you are all out for standing ovations and outstretched hands. You'll spend a sunny morning on the same sides of the table arguing the case between two pins and one and come back happily in the afternoon; when it happens to suit you, you'll put on any kind of act providing that you think it'll *work*. Start roaring out for marches, demonstrations in the streets and barricades and bloody flags and who knows what. All the messiahs of your own voices. The only peace you ever make is abusing everyone. Oh yes, my friends, you are a pair of strange ones.

BRUTUS: Come, come, Menenius. You know, and we know, that you'll be better remembered as an after-dinner speaker in the provinces rather than a serious politician in the Capitol.

MENENIUS: Even priests have to mock sometimes when they're confronted with the truly insignificant absurd. Well, I suppose you must be saying, still saying, that Marcius is proud; who at the merest calculation is worth more than you and all your predecessors since I can bother to remember. Perhaps the best of them might have inherited the skills of an executioner and that's about the lot. Good night, my friends. More of your conversation at this time of night would honestly make my brain reel; like a shepherd with a lot of drunken sheep to round up. I hope I haven't been too open. I don't *think* I have.

(*He gets up and leaves BRUTUS and SICINIUS alone in their chairs.*)

SICINIUS: People like him are only open behind closed doors.

(*BRUTUS takes out a sheet of paper and hands it to SICINIUS.*)

BRUTUS: Caius Marcius is coming home.

SICINIUS: I see. He'll have more cause than ever to strut about.

Scene 9

Airport near Rome. MENENIUS, ATTENDANTS, POLICEMEN, etc. Enter VOLUMNIA, VIRGILIA and VALERIA.

VOLUMNIA: Menenius, my dear, good friend. Marcius, my boy Marcius is on his way. He's coming home.

MENENIUS: Almost here. (*He looks up.*)

VOLUMNIA: And, Menenius, look at the crowds here to greet him, all along the route from Rome, as well as here!

MENENIUS: I know. And thank heaven for them. (*He embraces VOLUMNIA.*) Hooray. Marcius coming home.

VOLUMNIA: Look, here's a letter from him! The State's got another, his wife another; and, oh, I think there's one at home for you.

MENENIUS: At my house. Those fools must have made me miss it. I'll dash home after, make no mistake. I feel a new man, already. He is the best cure there is for any of us. Aches, pains or what you will. Is he well?

VIRGILIA: Oh, no, no, no.

VOLUMNIA: If he isn't, we'll take care of him and thank heavens we can.

MENENIUS: If it's not too bad this time.

VOLUMNIA: This is the third time he has come home to all this.

MENENIUS: I understand he salted Aufidius's tail for him.

VOLUMNIA: Titus Lartius says they got barrel to barrel but Aufidius got off.

MENENIUS: Not too soon, I'll bet. We must see that a full
     statement is made to the Senate before any questioning
     in the middle of all this.
VOLUMNIA: Let's look out for him. Yes, yes, yes. The
     Senate has had the General's report *and* my son's part in it.
VALERIA: Isn't it exciting! Where can we see best?
MENENIUS: Exciting! Yes, and well-sweated for.
VIRGILIA: If only it all goes well.
VOLUMNIA: Well? How else *can* it.
MENENIUS:(*To the tribunes, who have appeared.*) Just in
     time, my good friends. He's almost here. Where is he
     wounded?
VOLUMNIA: All over. They'll see.
VIRGILIA: (*Looking up at the sky.*) Not if I can help it.
VALERIA: One in the neck and two in the thigh I was told –
VOLUMNIA: Twenty-five before he ever started this
     campaign.
MENENIUS: Here he comes.
VIRGILIA: Where! Where!
MENENIUS: Just listen to that noise.
VIRGILIA: Damn the noise. Where is he?
VOLUMNIA: The cause of all this?   ˙
     (*The airport has gone wild with shouting and chanting.*)
VIRGILIA: And the tears he's left behind him.
VOLUMNIA: Not Marcius. *They* brought their deaths on
     them*selves*. He's the arm, if you like, not all of it, mind.
VIRGILIA: Nor heart, I should hope.
     (*Shouts and some confusion. COMINIUS and LARTIUS
     enter. Between them, discreetly but dashingly uniformed, is
     CORIOLANUS, accompanied by MEDICAL ORDERLIES,
     OFFICIALS, etc. Shouts of 'Caius Marcius', 'Lord Marcius
     of Corioli,' 'Corio-lan-us! Corio-lan-us!'.*)
CORIOLANUS: Are they all gone mad or what? That will
     do, I think. I've seen enough sickening things today;
     even for my stomach.
COMINIUS: Your mother's here.
CORIOLANUS: Oh, I know you're all overjoyed –
VOLUMNIA: Don't be modest, of all things; my
     by-rights-gentle Marcius; Caius who always truly
     'deserved'. And now you receive it; however brief it may

turn out to be, however much of a one night stand; it's
yours, and yours by your own efforts. But, Caius, no,
what is it we must call you now? Oh, here's your wife.
Now the Lady –

CORIOLANUS: I've seen and done bad things.

MENENIUS: No, no. You are tired, you need rest; make
some space there!

CORIOLANUS: Valeria, my dear, forgive me.

VOLUMNIA: I don't know what to say. Cominius, welcome
back, all of you.

MENENIUS: Yes, all of you. It's a sad day and a good, for
all that. Anyone here will see that.

COMINIUS: Quite so. Make way along there. Make a path.

CORIOLANUS (*To VOLUMNIA and VIRGILIA.*) Here!
Both of you. Before I ever get home there are people I've
got to see. Of course. It just has to be done.

VOLUMNIA: Today, everything I have ever wanted is true;
yours and mine; so what can anything else matter? There
is only one thing left for Rome to offer you and, after
this, I can't see them refusing it you.

CORIOLANUS: You have an instinct in these things,
matters, Mother.

COMINIUS: Time for us to get off to the Capitol.
(*In some confusion and clamour, as before, they go, leaving
SICINIUS and BRUTUS.*)

BRUTUS: For a few hours, he'll be different from the rest of
us. Apparently. Until it turns out, is made out, different.

SICINIUS: Just as you say. But with such supporters,
who needs –

BRUTUS: Enemies... True.

SICINIUS: People in Rome don't forget their fathers and
grandfathers on account of one day's bit of circus.
They're familiar enough with all this bit. They're just as
quick to be antagonised.

BRUTUS: I've heard him say enough times, and you too,
that he'll never 'put himself up to the mob' – quick
though he is to use 'em when it suits him. *I* can't see him
putting himself up to please. Can you? Unless appearing,

mark, *appearing* to displease, when the wind's in the right
place and then only then.

SICINIUS: Right, then let's make sure of it.

BRUTUS: That everyone is quite certain in their own
minds what he really means and thinks of them.

SICINIUS: He will. They will know. He'll see to that. The
rest is up to us.

(*Enter a MESSENGER.*) What is it?

MESSENGER: You're to go to the Capitol. Marcius is up
for Consul already. The returns are overwhelmingly in
his favour. I'm astonished you're not there.

SICINIUS: We know. You forget. We have been
there before.

(*They go out.*)

Scene 10

*Rome. A public place. Outcry. Two senior POLICE OFFICERS
conduct the crowd and observe.*

SECOND POLICE OFFICER: They all say Coriolanus
will have his way, in spite of all this.

FIRST POLICE OFFICER: Oh, he's brave enough and
clever enough. But is he clever enough – he loves no one
here today, that's for sure. If any day. And shows it
what's more.

SECOND POLICE OFFICER: There have been plenty
enough in the past to govern the people without *liking*
them; let alone loving them. They've flattered without
even hating them, like Coriolanus does.

FIRST POLICE OFFICER: No one can hate so
spectacularly without being tied up by love somewhere.

SECOND POLICE OFFICER: Who knows? It'll end soon
enough. In the meantime, we've enough on *our* hands to
see that he gets a safe escort while he's with us to still
need it.

(*Enter the PATRICIANS, and the tribunes of the people;
they are moving forward and are just held back as
CORIOLANUS, MENENIUS and COMINIUS – now*

*dressed as a Consul – enter. SICINIUS and BRUTUS
separate themselves and take up prominent positions by the
people of Rome.)*

MENENIUS: (*Silencing the crowd, more or less.*) Having done
with – yes, done with I say, done with the Volsces, and
apart from recalling Titus Lartius, the main business, the
only truly pleasurable one in all this business, it should
be publicly spelled out what part was played in the very
best of that tragic business by: Caius Marcius
Coriolanus.

(*Some cries of: CORIO-LAN-US!*)

Which is why we are rallied here together; all sections
and representatives of the people of Rome; patricians,
so-called plebians, tribunes of the people, consuls, we are
all, yes, all I say, *citizens of Rome.* And who is not proud
to say so?

SICINIUS: Let's hear from Coriolanus himself on that.

FIRST SENATOR: You speak first, Cominius. Leave
nothing out. (*To the TRIBUNES.*) Let him have the floor,
and then it will be your turn.

SICINIUS: We are here to listen as well as say our piece.
Always have been.

BRUTUS: We can't always be expected though to control
carefully calculated incitements to the ordinary people;
the Heart of Rome itself. That's *your* time-honoured
occupation; indeed, obsession.

MENENIUS: That's not on. Not on at all. I'd rather you'd
not said that. On second thoughts –

SICINIUS: As always –

MENENIUS: I'm glad you did. Will you allow Cominius
to speak?

BRUTUS: Certainly. I was merely pointing out that you
cannot blame us for not having the resources to control
situations created by yourselves.

MENENIUS: He has never had anything but the love of
his country and of you all as his first thought. Tell 'em,
Cominius.

(*CORIOLANUS rises and offers to go away.*)

MENENIUS: No, stay where you are.

CORIOLANUS: Please to forgive me. I'd rather go
back to it all than hear it gone over and how it
came about.

BRUTUS: Sir, I hope nothing we've said has upset your
stomach for these very typical Roman occasions. Every
voice must let itself be heard.

CORIOLANUS: *Heard!* You call slogans and horses
charged by your waving banners, being heard! I've got
as much stomach for all of that as –

MENENIUS: Sit down!

CORIOLANUS: I'd rather sit at home and think; picking
my cat's fleas for him than go in for whatever you call
this – making speeches about what I may or may not
have done...
(*Exit CORIOLANUS.*)

MENENIUS: Cominius!
(*Some boos and cat calls follow CORIOLANUS.*)

COMINIUS: Now, now –

VOICE: Speak up!

COMINIUS: I am here. What can I say of one man? When
all you understand is parties, factions, invented plots,
insights, misbegotten, slavering, from the inside reports.
You talk of pride, some of you. It *is* one part of that man.
I couldn't be that man, but I wish that one of you could
even be a little less than one part of that man. His flaws
are lasting monuments already, while your well-planned
assessments and schemes and developments are brought
into this world like the bright, deformed slums they were
always; conceived in clever ignorance. He doesn't want
anything –

SICINIUS: He's got it already –

COMINIUS: What he was born with...

MENENIUS: Call him back. Call Coriolanus back.
(*Dissension and indecision in the crowd.*)

SECOND POLICE OFFICER: Here he is, sir.
(*Enter CORIOLANUS.*)

MENENIUS: The Senate, Coriolanus, *will* be pleased to
make you consul.

CORIOLANUS: As you wish.

MENENIUS: The only thing left is to make your platform acceptable all round.

CORIOLANUS: Please, I do ask you not even to try to do that. I can't play kiss my arse and ask for favours or votes of confidence. Not even to make them feel the illusion of power, or the ritual bestowings of it. Please, let me out of this one.

SICINIUS: Sir, you must speak to the people; the people of Rome. Speak yourself to them, that's all they ask of you.

CORIOLANUS: Must I? Must I? Then I think it's time I must *not*.

SICINIUS: They have a right at least to all the forms.

MENENIUS: Do as they say. We all have to do it.

CORIOLANUS: 'Having to'. 'Forms' may not necessarily be 'rights'.

BRUTUS: (*To SICINIUS.*) You hear that.

CORIOLANUS: To have to say I did this for you and then that. What I had to for them without pain to myself.

MENENIUS: Don't make an issue of this. It's everyday coinage – or conversion, change over; redevelopment; rethinking; streamlining; adjusting to new needs, circumstances – you know the phrases.

CORIOLANUS: I do. I am not obliged to *use* them.

MENENIUS: You are, my friend, or you will be. Tribunes of the People, you see our choice.

SICINIUS: We do.

SENATORS: CORIO-LAN-US!

(*They go out, leaving tribunes and stragglers. Band plays. CROWD starts to break up.*)

BRUTUS: You see where his mind's going?

SICINIUS: Do you think we are the only ones? He will have to put his case to them; *and* tout around for seals of approval from all kinds of places he affects to detest.

BRUTUS: Come. We've got a campaign of our own to work out.

Scene 11

Rome. A public place near the forum. An election van with hailer on top and CORIOLANUS posters. Enter several CITIZENS.

FIRST CITIZEN: If he's not so stubborn and can bring himself to listen as well as talk, and talk *to* us, I don't see why he shouldn't have our votes.

SECOND CITIZEN: That's for all of us to make up our minds.

THIRD CITIZEN: I'd say we could do worse.
(Enter CORIOLANUS, unobtrusively dressed, rather like the CITIZENS, with MENENIUS.)
There he is, looking like any man in the street. Let's split up and go up to him in ones and twos – on the quiet. Everyone can put a question to him about his own problems. That way he can't complain of facing an incoherent, unreasoning or unlistening mob.

MENENIUS: My dear chap, we've all had to do it in the past, not only now; the greatest men in Rome have cheerfully subjected themselves to it.

CORIOLANUS: 'Cheerfully subjected'. What do I say to them? It makes my tongue all ulcerated to think of myself.

MENENIUS: Do not think of your*self* and don't abuse your tongue or you'll end up with even more than ulcers in your hands. Think of Rome – of Rome alone. You need its popular support – to begin with – not just the respect of a few of us.

CORIOLANUS: Popular support. I'd rather be forgotten by them all.

MENENIUS: You'll ruin everything. Think about it. Try speaking to them in an ordinary, friendly way. *(Goes out.)*

CORIOLANUS: No such thing.
(Three CITIZENS approach.)
Tell them I hope they've had their weekly bath and cleaned their teeth. Ah, here's a couple… You know why I'm standing about here?

THIRD CITIZEN: We do, sir. Some call it the 'hustings'.

CORIOLANUS: For my own ends.

SECOND CITIZEN: Your own?

CORIOLANUS: Not because I wish to stand up here in this ridiculous attitude.

THIRD CITIZEN: How's that?

CORIOLANUS: I was never one to approach the poor with appeals for charity.

THIRD CITIZEN: You must think that whatever we might choose to give you, we'd expect something in return.

CORIOLANUS: I'm prepared to go through this for your price; for a consul's life. And what would you say was that price?

FIRST CITIZEN: The price is to ask for it kindly. Understandingly, helpful; uncondescending.

CORIOLANUS: Kindly? I *have* been kindly, as you call it, and what else, dispersed more understanding, helpfulness than you've had public benefits.

SECOND CITIZEN: Well, I'll take a chance on you.

CORIOLANUS: A convert, sir. There's a couple.

THIRD CITIZEN: This doesn't seem the right way to me to go about it.

SECOND CITIZEN: Well, there it is.

(*They go out and are replaced by two more CITIZENS. CORIOLANUS speaks into his loud hailer on the top of the van.*)

CORIOLANUS: This is Coriolanus, your candidate for the consulship.

FIRST CITIZEN: You've done all right in some things but very good in others.

CORIOLANUS: Ah! An enigmatist!

FIRST CITIZEN: Oh, you've mopped up the troubles overseas in *your* way. But you don't *do* anything, let alone care anything for us, your own ordinary people.

CORIOLANUS: You should think the more of me for it, for not being indiscriminate. Oh, I will make the right noises to my brothers, my comrades, my people. Will they think the better of me for it? So it seems. They demand reason, reassurances, promises and: policies, those policies you love so dearly; so if you prefer that to my private voice, you shall have it; for I'm not without skill in showing off my policies – like a dancing girl wriggling on the Capitol in front of your tired, old, eager eyes. I can strip off before your very eyes and dissemble very nicely – if a cavorting eunuch's what you're after. *And I* should have known: you are! *I* am your man! Make *me* your consul!

SECOND CITIZEN: What's he on about? We only want to *hear* from you. Wages, prices, schemes, rehabilitation work, hours, conditions.

CORIOLANUS: You shall, my friend.

FIRST CITIZEN: Hear, hear.

SECOND CITIZEN: What are you 'hear, hearing'?

CORIOLANUS: I will deal with these things. And sharply. But you don't want to stand listening to *me.*

BOTH: Good luck, mate. (*They go out.*)

CORIOLANUS: Good luck, mate... Voice of my heart! I'd rather be shot at than go through this knocking on doors for a pair of powerful boots; or scuffling in the streets of Rome. Begging from every Tired Tom and Dozey Dick who wants to put in his few miserable pence. Tradition, the law demands it of us all. Anything can be allowed to happen or rise up if it's only in the name of common tradition. Rather than that, they can stuff their boots up to their elbow and let 'em stay there.
(*Enter three more CITIZENS. CORIOLANUS picks up the hailer.*)
Can you hear me? Can you? Hear me? Well, I am peddling myself, and I need *your* voices. Not only mine – to make me consul.
(*Some cheers. Then enter MENENIUS and the tribunes of the people.*)

CORIOLANUS: You hear that. The People's voice. Isn't that a sound? Enough to gag a man's bowels!

SICINIUS: What's that?

CORIOLANUS: Oh, and women too, madam, or what it is I should call you?

MENENIUS: (*Hurriedly, seeing trouble.*) You've done
well. And the tribunes here will endorse you. The rest
will be formality, I tell you. Then off to the Senate at
long last.

CORIOLANUS: Is this true?

SICINIUS: You have played your part. You will get your
consulship by the consent of the people.

CORIOLANUS: Where next? The Senate House?

SICINIUS The Senate House.

CORIOLANUS: Can I get these things off now?

SICINIUS: You may.

CORIOLANUS: I'll do that right away and feel myself
again – if I'm still there.

MENENIUS: I'll come with you. Will *you* come?

BRUTUS: We'll stay down here a while.

SICINIUS: Goodbye, Coriolanus.
(*CORIOLANUS and MENENIUS go out.*)
It's all but in his pocket now.

BRUTUS: He didn't give much away. (*Enter the
PLEBIANS.*)

SICINIUS: Well, is he our man?

FIRST CITIZEN: He's got our vote.

BRUTUS: Let's hope he deserves it.

SECOND CITIZEN: Hear, hear, to that. But it seemed to
me, he didn't think much of anyone, not himself even.
He poked fun at everyone, everything.

THIRD CITIZEN: Right. He was having it over us
quite openly.

FIRST CITIZEN: No. It is his manner, his way of speaking
we didn't catch. He doesn't mean it.

SECOND CITIZEN: Well, you're the only one to think so.
He hardly bothered to explain himself.

SICINIUS: But he must have done.

ALL: No. No. What did we hear!

THIRD CITIZEN: All he talked about was something
about all being, I don't remember – being condemned to
moments of isolating oneself, at one time or another in
one's life. But what has he to *SAY*! That's what I'd like to

find out. All I know is that he wants to be consul. Some
grudging sweet talk all round and then that's that! Was
this not a mockery!

(*Cheers.*)

SICINIUS: Either you were mistaken or, if you were not,
then why did you pledge him your support?

BRUTUS: Couldn't you have said to him that he's the same
man he's always been? That he is, has been, and always
will he against our kind!

(*Roars.*)

You should have told him each and every one of the
things he stands for. Not changed! Do you believe:
changed! You are conned and conned easily and well he
knows it.

SICINIUS: You know his temper. Why didn't you trample
on it? That would have shown you: that would have seen
the end of *his* election.

BRUTUS: Didn't you see one outstretched palm and the
other raising up his finger at you? When he *wanted* you!
And do you think he'll treat you any better for this
trick? Wasn't there one doubtful soul among you?

SICINIUS: Well, what do you say now?

THIRD CITIZEN: It's still not fixed. There's time yet to
reverse it; if we've a mind to it.

SECOND CITIZEN: Well?

(*Cheers and acclaim.*)

FIRST CITIZEN: And I'll double that show of hands
in hours.

BRUTUS: Get to it then. Tell your friends they've chosen
the wrong consul; who's against all they've fought for
and against. They have some liberties, let them
brandish them.

SICINIUS: Get them altogether. And when they've thought
better of it and realised what they've done, put him to
the real test. Smoke him out. He is there for it. So go to
it. Let him show, and show to *everyone*, what his real
opinion is of you.

BRUTUS: Forgive us for having seemed to stand aside. But
the time came for you to act on your own.

SICINIUS: Yes. Blame it on *us*. But, in the meantime,
    you've found your own true voice.
BRUTUS: Oh, say what you like about *us*. Say we talked
    you into it.
SICINIUS: Change your minds and tell him so and *why*!
    (*Roars. The PLEBIANS go out.*)
BRUTUS: Let them go. It's best to take a risk at this stage.
SICINIUS: We'd better go to the Capitol. In the forefront.

Scene 12

*Rome. A conference room. Into the room with its long table and rows
of chairs come CORIOLANUS, MENENIUS, SENATORS,
COMINIUS and LARTIUS.*

CORIOLANUS: So Aufidius has made some more new
    ground.
LARTIUS: He has. Which was why we had to come to
    some kind of terms quicker.
CORIOLANUS: So then, so then, we are back where we
    started except the Volscians are no doubt better off than
    ever and ready to start up the whole thing again, when it
    suits them.
COMINIUS: They are worn out, Lord Consul. I hardly
    think we shall see those banners wave again in our
    lifetime.
CORIOLANUS: Did you see Aufidius?
LARTIUS: We had a pre-arranged meeting in secret. He was
    full of bile for the Volscians giving up the town so easily
    as he seemed to think. Now he's gone back to Antium.
CORIOLANUS: Did he speak about me?
LARTIUS: He did indeed.
CORIOLANUS: How? What?
LARTIUS: The times he had met you; of all the things he'd
    pawn in order to get you.
CORIOLANUS: And he's staying at Antium, you say?
LARTIUS: Antium. If only I could be given the excuse to
    go and get him back.
    (*Enter SICINIUS and BRUTUS.*)

SICINIUS: Stay where you are.

CORIOLANUS: What is this?

ERUTUS: I am warning you. It will be dangerous for you
   to go out of here.

CORIOLANUS: What has happened?

MENENIUS: The facts?

COMINIUS: Is the vote not as good as his? All but the
   counting?

BRUTUS: No, Cominius.

CORIOLANUS: So these were children's voices?

FIRST SENATOR: Out of the way, tribunes. He's to go to
   his place.

BRUTUS: They've been roused up against him.

SICINIUS: We wouldn't advise it.

CORIOLANUS: Is this your herd? Has the cat given back
   their tongues? Their mouths seem empty enough; but
   own up aren't you their teeth? Haven't *you* set them on?

MENENIUS: Calm, do be calm.

CORIOLANUS: This is all a trumped-up thing; and it will
   get bigger. First it was to flout the law and when that
   wasn't frightening enough for you, you take on yourselves
   to maim and injure anyone in sight. And why? Because
   policy – yes, policy – dominates and is...wonderfully
   afraid. That's your game, isn't it?

BRUTUS: Not a worse one than the way you go
   about yours.

CORIOLANUS: Why should I elect to be a consul? Let life
   do me so much ill that I'll end up like you and be a
   tribune.

SICINIUS: These are your true colours.

MENENIUS: Let's try to be calm.

COMINIUS: People feel they have been abused, stirred up,
   led to believe things that were not so. This lack of
   openness doesn't become Rome. Nor does Coriolanus
   deserve to be brushed aside.

CORIOLANUS: Talk to me of wages, prices! I spoke to
   them once and I will again.

MENENIUS: Not now, not now.

FIRST SENATOR: Not in your present mood.

CORIOLANUS: *Now*; *I will*! 'My good friends', I crave their pardon each and every one of them, changeable, aggressive, craven, every one of them. Don't let them think of me as a flatterer and therefore fit to govern them. Let's not throw away everything we have sown and tended for a few rebellious weeds, and weeds I do mean, by letting them in too far.

MENENIUS: Well, no more.

FIRST SENATOR: No, no more words for heaven's sake.

CORIOLANUS: What! No more! Why shouldn't my lungs be allowed to go on coining words until they burst, as sure as hell they will?

BRUTUS: You talk of people as if you were God, expressly brought up to punish as if you'd no diseases of your own at all.

SICINIUS: The sooner it's made clear to them, the better.

MENENIUS: What, what! His anger?

CORIOLANUS: Anger? If I were as patient as my deepest sleep, dear God, it would still be from my *mind*.

SICINIUS: Then it's a mind that shall stay where it is –

CORIOLANUS: Is! 'Shall stay where it is'? Did you hear this frightening black-faced lady! Did you hear!

COMINIUS: She was out of order.

CORIOLANUS: 'Shall'! Oh, you nice, foolish men. You plodding, reckless Senators. This lady here has so many heads she cannot live with them all, which is why she chooses to lose them in a mob of others. If you think power lies there, then give in to it now. If not, do something about it and at once. Would you let them pitch their 'shall' against yours? This popular 'shall' against the gentlest and most civilised society the world has seen! It makes my bones ache to see such a situation; when two sides are both too weak to assume supremacy; and how revolution will come between the two of them and destroy the lot.

COMINIUS: We must be off.

MENENIUS: Yes, no more of that.

CORIOLANUS: I'll give my reasons when asked for 'em.
What can you give to the Siciniuses of Rome to satisfy
their prudish imaginations? 'We are the strongest
because we are the most, to hell with the best, we do not
acknowledge such a possibility. What we make, we shall
employ.' Not invent, mark you, what we *make*, look into
the future to. They talk of this sweat and that's their most
important product – and they smell it over half the
world. Well, let them take it over; let it *be* theirs!

MENENIUS: That's enough.

BRUTUS: Enough for us!

CORIOLANUS: No, not enough for me. Well, let's get to
your policies; the ones without purpose, except to
indulge the worst of you and pacify the rest.

SICINIUS: Your mouth is your undoing, my friend. Have
you not heard of such a thing as reticence in politicking?

CORIOLANUS: I have not learned from you. You are too
trivial for reticence; otherwise you would disappear up
your own supporters. In a rebellion like this, we must
live under the law or there will be no life for the most
of us.

SICINIUS: Or change it.

CORIOLANUS: Change it! Administer it. You could not
own a stall in the market without state assistance.

SICINIUS: This a consul? No!
(*Enter an AEDILE – a sort of people's policeman.*)
(*To AEDILE.*) Take him. Get the city all together.
(*Exit AEDILE.*)

CORIOLANUS: Go on, get them together, 'policeman' –
policeman of the piss poor! Get off out of it, hairy
charm-pits.

PATRICIANS: We'll stand surety for him.
(*The tribunes attack COMINIUS. CORIOLANUS
intervenes, grabbing them.*)

CORIOLANUS: Get off before I play marbles with the two
of you!

SICINIUS: Help!
(*Confusion as police and troops arrive. Roars and singing
from outside.*)

Scene 13

A public square. Crowds and noise. As before, only more so, from Rome.

ALL: Tribunes! – Patricians! – Citizens! – Ay, ay! Sicinius! Brutus! Coriolanus! Workers! People!

MENENIUS: Will you listen. I can't make myself heard if you won't listen. I can't speak. You, tribunes, speak to them. Hold back, Coriolanus. Sicinius, you are the one they want to hear!

SICINIUS: Comrades! People! Listen!

CROWD: Go on then! Get on with it! Let's hear some bit of sense. (*Etc.*)

SICINIUS: Just this: you're about to lose your freedom, that's all. Marcius will have the lot off you. Yes, Caius Marcius, whom you even chose to elect as consul!

MENENIUS: Now then, now. This is the way to rioting, not public discussion of the issue.

FIRST SENATOR: This way we'll just end up a flattened city and nothing else.

SICINIUS: What's the city but the people in it?

ALL: The people are the city. We are the people – CITY! We are the people – CITY! We are the people – CITY! (*They are held back. Just.*)

BRUTUS: And who represents them, that city?

ALL: You do! CITY! CITY! CITY!

MENENIUS: And so you will go on doing.

COMINIUS: This is the way to bring us all down to a new age of desolation and darkness.

SICINIUS: You hear that? Darkness he calls it. What is that to us?

ALL: Light. L-I-G-H-T! Light!

BRUTUS: MARCIUS out!

SICINIUS: You hear that!

ALL: MAR-CI-US OUT!

SICINIUS: Get him.

ALL: (*CITIZENS.*) Get, down, MARCIUS. Out, Marcius, O-U-T, *out!*

MENENIUS: Give me a word, I ask you!

BRUTUS: We know your 'old school'. Grab him.

MENENIUS: Someone help MARCIUS.

CROWD: Get him! Get him! (*Etc.*)
> (*Confusion as people and policemen, troops confront each other. Howling, people trod underfoot. The crowd surges forward but is scattered.*)

CORIOLANUS: We are not without friends.

COMINIUS: Let's get out of it.
> (*They go under escort.*)

MENENIUS: Go home. All of you. In the name of Rome and your children and their children. We shall sit down and talk this out or give up everything.

SICINIUS: (*To MOB.*) What? Coriolanus? Well?

MENENIUS: Your consul.

SICINIUS: What consul?

BRUTUS: He, consul?

CROWD: No, no, no, NO. Out, out, out out!
> (*MENENIUS goes out.*)

SICINIUS: Oh, we'll talk.
> (*Cheers from MOB.*)

Scene 14

Rome. The house of CORIOLANUS. Enter CORIOLANUS with MENENIUS, SENATORS.

CORIOLANUS: My mother's disapproval *does* surprise me. Even though it's so obvious by now. She was always the first to support me – even in her best misunderstanding.
(*Enter VOLUMNIA.*)
Well, now, Mother, I'm talking of you. Why do you want me to be milder then? You, you to want me false to my nature? Rather than take a stab at what I am?

VOLUMNIA: Oh, Caius, I want only what is best for you and what's best for you must be best for Rome.

CORIOLANUS: Oh, enough of that!

VOLUMNIA: You can be the man you are without striving this much. You would have done better to show less, not more.

CORIOLANUS: Let 'em hang.

VOLUMNIA: Oh, and burn too.

MENENIUS: Come, come, you're indiscreet to the point of lunacy. But there's still time to make amends. There always is.

SENATOR: If you don't we shall all be brought down, if the city itself doesn't disappear for good.

VOLUMNIA: Listen to them, Caius. My heart's just the same as yours, but its detachment's still there –

MENENIUS: Well said. He must address himself to the situation as it is, not as he would have it.

CORIOLANUS: What do you want me to do?

MENENIUS: Take it all back and do it with conviction. They are not fooled easily.

CORIOLANUS: For *them.* I could not do it for my wife, my son, my life. Would you get me to do it for *them*?

VOLUMNIA: You are too passionate and too pedantic with it. Like, they say wrongly, women – only it's not so.

CORIOLANUS: Too passionate or too pedantic?

VOLUMNIA: Neither. I won't argue with you in this mood. But I've heard you say yourself honour and policy can go together without necessarily debasing one another.

CORIOLANUS: I must have been drunk, ironic; both; that or you weren't listening to my real voice.

MENENIUS: Listen to her.

VOLUMNIA: After all, if you can see your way to bluffing so successfully in war, why not now, when far more's at stake?

CORIOLANUS: Why pursue it?

VOLUMNIA: Because now is not the time to indulge in passion but talk in terms that everyone will accept and understand. There's no dishonour in bringing the city to just terms merely by using the right form of words. How can you play emotion with so much *future*? I would do *far* more. For your wife, your son, these upright senators, all of them. Do you want just to impress louts with your intransigence? They don't know what it means!

MENENIUS: She's right. But we must make a move while there's still time.

VOLUMNIA: My son. Do it. We, who know you the most, we'll know what you are doing *and* why.

MENENIUS: Do as she says, and we still have a chance…

VOLUMNIA: Go and look as if you have been overruled. It's not beyond you.

(*Enter COMINIUS.*)

COMINIUS: It's all uproar. Only Coriolanus can damp it down. Even so, it looks like being too late.

MENENIUS: A few words… The right *appearance.*

VOLUMNIA: He must, he will. I beg you, say you will…

CORIOLANUS: Go out there to lie? A lie that's *mine* for always? Well, I'll do it. I'll put on the right face, the familiar expressions, the flattened, conciliatory vowels. I will, what is it, agree, no, not agree, *plead* for arbitration.

COMINIUS: We'll all help you.

VOLUMNIA: You have done things before you hated. Do this, just for this last time.

CORIOLANUS: Well then, I must do it. Don't press your point, Mother, I'll dissemble better than the best of you.

VOLUMNIA: Do as you like.

(*Exit VOLUMNIA.*)

COMINIUS: The tribunes are waiting. Be prepared indeed to conciliate, be mild. They are watching for every flicker. Heaven knows what new things they've up their sleeves.

CORIOLANUS: Right. 'Mildly' is the word. Let's get it over with. I have a few unplayed tricks of my own.

MENENIUS: But mildly, remember.

CORIOLANUS: Well, mildly be it then. Mildly.

Scene 15

Rome. The Forum. SICINIUS and BRUTUS raised above the MOB. Crescendo as they appear above everyone.

MOB: We want Marcius!
We want Marcius!
We want Marcius!

BRUTUS: He's coming.

SICINIUS: Who with?

BRUTUS: Menenius and his old mob.

SICINIUS: Have you a count of votes?

BRUTUS: It's all done.

SICINIUS: Each area?

BRUTUS: Every one. That matters.

SICINIUS: Get them all in close. And when I say: 'It's the voice of the people' – whether it be for a fine, banishment, or death; if I say 'Fine' yell 'Fine', if 'Let him have it', then 'Let him have it', 'Kill him' and so on. Understood? Death in revolution can't be called 'murder' afterwards. So, look to it.

BRUTUS: Will do. The stewards know already. If he's not on the boil already, they'll soon turn him up. He's not used to being answered in his own insulting coin. Once we've got him good and riled, there's no going back. He'll put his heart, where his neck is, on the chopper. (*Enter CORIOLANUS, MENENIUS, COMINIUS and others.*)

SICINIUS: So, there he is at long last.

MENENIUS: Calm, now.

CORIOLANUS: I have promised. I will try: for Rome.

FIRST SENATOR: Amen, amen.

MENENIUS: Good lad!

SICINIUS: Listen to me, hear out your tribunes. Calm it down. Now. Please. I ask you!

CORIOLANUS: First, let me speak.

SICINIUS: Well now.

BRUTUS: His lordship's come to talk to you!

CORIOLANUS: Do we, can we, come to some terms in, in this place?

SICINIUS: I merely ask that you put your case to these citizens who've gathered here, with their lawful officers. And that you accept their reply. That's all.

CORIOLANUS: Very well.

MENENIUS: You see? He's served us all in our different ways.

CORIOLANUS: Only with laughter?

MENENIUS: Just so. He doesn't mince words. And not a
   bad thing in these times, *I* say!

COMINIUS: Get on with it.

CORIOLANUS: Why have you changed your minds and
   turned against me so late in the game?

SICINIUS: You tell *us*!

CORIOLANUS: I'll try.

SICINIUS: They've discovered at last that all moderation
   would end with you.

CORIOLANUS: And *you*!

SICINIUS: I love this city. Most of all, I love its people.
   You are its traitor; their traitor and they have found
   you out.

CORIOLANUS: How? Traitor!

MENENIUS: Mild, mild, you said.

CORIOLANUS: Call me traitor, you dead droppings of old
   cant. You lie. You lie in your green teeth!

SICINIUS: You hear him? Such moderation...

MOB: *Do* him. Do him! Kill him! Kill him! Kill... (*Etc.*)

SICINIUS: Enough, cowards. Enough, for we've seen
   enough. Haven't we seen *enough* of this – MAN!

BRUTUS: It's true he's done some things for Rome.

CORIOLANUS: What do you know about it?

BRUTUS: I know what I'm talking about.

CORIOLANUS: You!

MENENIUS: So much for your promise to your mother.

COMINIUS: Now, listen a moment –

CORIOLANUS: I wouldn't take *their* say-so for NUPPENCE
   one way or the other. I wouldn't give 'em the sweat from
   my balls.

SICINIUS: Let him go before he's killed – and it wouldn't
   be unjust –

MOB: Send him off! Take him off! Get lost! And for
   damned good and forever... (*Etc.*)

COMINIUS: Listen!

SICINIUS: You heard the verdict clear enough. Again?
   (*Roar.*)
   Right. He's done for. No more talk. We have heard it all
   before from your like.

BRUTUS: Right. That's it then.

MOB: That's it! That's it! (*Etc.*)

CORIOLANUS: You common cry of curs. You take up my
air. Banish me? *I* banish *you*! Stay here in your slum. And
strike. Communicate. Get shaken with rumours; fads;
modishness; greed; fashion; your clannishness; your
lives in depth. May you, but you won't, one minute of
that depth, know desolation. May your enemies barter
and exchange you coolly in their own better
market-places... I have seen the *future* here... and it
doesn't work! *I* turn my back. There is a world *elsewhere*!
(*He goes off, borne away by his supporters and sorely harassed
escort. CORIOLANUS sings down at them a parody of 'The
Red Flag'.*)
'The working class
Can kiss my arse
And keep their Red
Rag flying high.'
(*He is swept off, pursued by the furious MOB.*)

End of Act One.

ACT TWO

Scene 1

Airport. CORIOLANUS, VOLUMNIA, VIRGILIA, MENENIUS, COMINIUS. CORIOLANUS is embracing VIRGILIA.

CORIOLANUS: Come, that's enough. Farewells really are a lifetime. Come along, Mother, you've always been only too good on these occasions – away to school, the army, death beds, funerals, you've been an admirable Goodbyer. I thought you'd taught me pretty well.

VIRGILIA: Oh, Caius, Caius.

CORIOLANUS: I beg you –

VOLUMNIA: You giggled when I used to talk of red pestilence; the trades of Rome; all occupations gone but war and bargaining and faction –

CORIOLANUS: What's this? You should miss me when I'm *here*, not gone or about to go. Be the same as ever was, Mother. Cominius, my friend, this will all change and sort itself out as it has before... Goodbye, Virgilia... Menenius, soppy old thing, I always knew it. My old chief, my friend. Look after them all. I know you will. Mother, you know that my worst setbacks have stirred you on. Not cast you down. Don't think I go my own way easily or lightly. More talked about and forgotten... and not seen. I will do more than the usual, as you know, unless I'm sold out, who knows how?

VOLUMNIA: My very first son, where will you go? Take Cominius with you. Make some plan first rather than expose yourself to every wildcat waiting in every corner for you.

CORIOLANUS: Oh, God!

COMINIUS: I'll come with you. Somewhere we can hole up and draw up a proper campaign. So, when the time comes, as it will, when they need you back, there'll be no other man left in the world they'll turn to. They'll soon see what's lacking in them.

CORIOLANUS: No, Cominius, it's too late for you to follow me on this kind of jaunt. Just see me off. Come, Virgilia, Mother, Menenius. Just see the going of me and go home for a gossip and a drink or two. You shall hear from me. And never any differently than before.

MENENIUS: Exactly. I still wish *I* were young enough to come with you.

CORIOLANUS: Give me your hand. Come.

(*They go out.*)

Scene 2

Rome. Airport. SICINIUS and BRUTUS.

SICINIUS: They can all go home. He's gone and that's that. The top brass are pretty fed up with us, but, of course, they've sided with him all along; *and* at his extremist, though they'd dare not say as much.

BRUTUS: Now we've shown the support we've got, we can afford to seem more amenable.

SICINIUS: We can *all* go home and say the great fanatic who represents no responsible opinion has gone and we are back to where we were and can start again.

BRUTUS: That's his mother.

(*Enter VOLUMNIA, VIRGILIA and MENENIUS.*)

SICINIUS: Let's avoid her.

BRUTUS: Why?

SICINIUS: They say she's gone quite cracked.

BRUTUS: They've seen us. Keep going.

VOLUMNIA: Ah, there you are. Your come-uppance hasn't been called yet, but it will.

MENENIUS: Don't raise your voice. It's pointless.

VOLUMNIA: Do you think I am not trying –
(*In tears.*) Or they'd *hear* –
No, you *will* hear.
(*To BRUTUS.*) Going?

VIRGILIA: (*To SICINIUS.*) Yes, and you stay too. I wish I could have said so to my husband.

SICINIUS: What are you then? Mankind? Or something?

VOLUMNIA: That was a shoddy answer. My father was
mankind, if you like. You think you have the wit to keep
my Coriolanus out of Rome, who has done more,
thought more, been more –
SICINIUS: Not that! God preserve us that!
VOLUMNIA: More than your old, reach-me-down words.
I tell you. I tell you what – no, go. No, you shall stay.
You are not fit to meet him face to face whatever world
you found yourselves in.
SICINIUS: So?
VIRGILIA: So? He'll see *you* out!
VOLUMNIA: Bastards and all. Oh, what has happened to
him!
MENENIUS: Come, come…
SICINIUS: It's a pity he did not go on as he seemed to
start – on all our behalves.
BRUTUS: It is.
VOLUMNIA: It is! It was you who roused them up. Like
tom cats in the night who know as little of what he is as
I know of what lies ahead of us.
BRUTUS: Let's go.
VOLUMNIA: Yes, you go! You must be feeling very brave
today. But before you do, listen to this: as far as all
Rome is finer than you each in your little houses, this
lady's husband is better than any one of you.
BRUTUS: Well, we'll go.
SICINIUS: Why stay to be harangued by a dotty
old woman!
(*Tribunes exit.*)
VOLUMNIA: And my fingers with you! If I had nothing
else to do but think of alternatives to *them*! If only
I could set eyes on them once a day, it might help.
MENENIUS: They got your message, madam. Shall we
dine together?
VOLUMNIA:I can't eat except what's in here for them.
Very well, let's get going. We can't stand wasting time.
MENENIUS: Oh, dear.
(*They all go.*)

Scene 3

Antium. Near AUFIDIUS's headquarters. CORIOLANUS comes out of a drab-looking pub, dressed like a working man. A MAN follows him out.

CORIOLANUS: Good evening to you.
MAN: And to you.
CORIOLANUS: Tell me, if it's possible, where's Aufidius?
MAN: Aufidius?
CORIOLANUS: He *is* in Antium?
MAN: Everyone knows that. He'll be having a right old carouse with the best of 'em tonight.
CORIOLANUS: Tell me, where can I make contact with him?
MAN: Who wants to know?
CORIOLANUS: Someone; someone uniquely placed to get him what he's always set his heart on.
   (*MAN hesitates then he scribbles on a piece of paper, which he hands to CORIOLANUS.*)
   Thank you.
MAN: Forget you saw me.
   (*He disappears into the shadows. CORIOLANUS reads the piece of paper.*)
CORIOLANUS: Here I am, hating my own birthplace and ending up in Autium with a slip of paper. Oh, world, what slippery terms! Oh, I can find this place. If he shoots me down, he'll have done well for himself. If not, *I* can do things for him even now.

Scene 4

Antium. A room in AUFIDIUS's headquarters. CORIOLANUS is being restrained by three of AUFIDIUS's men.

AUFIDIUS: Who the devil's this?
FIRST MAN: I'll beat the bejesus out of him.
AUFIDIUS: Who let him get in at all?
FIRST MAN: Nobody, Aufidius.
AUFIDIUS: Oh, nobody is it? Then nobody let go of him and nobody let him out! Where do you come from?

What do you want? Speak up. What's your name?

CORIOLANUS: (*Unmuffling.*) If, Tullus, you still can't
guess who I am, take me for what I am: necessity!

AUFIDIUS: Name?

CORIOLANUS: Not one that's liked much by the
Volscians; least of all by you.

AUFIDIUS: Your name. Your clothes don't fool me, but
I can't see the face.

CORIOLANUS: Then prepare yourself. Still not know?

AUFIDIUS: I've told you. Your name, damn you.

CORIOLANUS: Caius Marcius. Or, Coriolanus, to you.
For that's my name since I think we last had the pleasure.
That surname's all I have to show for the services I gave
to my grateful country. So much… A name for the
hatred you've lived off for the likes of me. A name…
Coriolanus. All that's left to me before being whooped
out of Rome. Which is how I end up here with you.
Oh, believe me, not to save my life, for this is the last
place I would come to if I were merely hanging on to
something I never had much care for and still less now.
I am here for, for miserable spite; no more no less. If
you want your revenge for Corioli, you *could* take it now.
Then you'd best do it now rather than gossip with me.
Otherwise, think how you can use me against your
enemy – against troops. Battalions of 'em. Even *you*
might do with *my* spleen. Think on it. Still, if the idea is
beyond your Volscian folk visions, it's beyond me too;
even the hatred I once felt for you and all your vicious
kind. There *is* nothing left but leading *your* kind.

AUFIDIUS: Oh, Marcius, Marcius! What are you doing to
me! From your lips. Here!
(*They embrace.*)
I loved my wife when I first clapped eyes on her, but my
heart's not run such a dance since she crossed my own
doorway. Marcius, Caius Marcius!
(*They embrace again.*)
Why, I tell you we shall put such a force in the field the
world will be *astonished.* I have dreamt of killing you
with my own hands so many times, I no longer even

wake up with the sweat unless my wife begs me to stop thrashing about. Marcius, if we had no other quarrel with Rome than that she'd slung you out, that, that would be enough for me. Come in, come in, meet everyone. We are making plans at the moment for the outskirts; if not actually Rome itself.

CORIOLANUS: God bless you.

AUFIDIUS: You are perfect. Perfect. Who knows better, *feels* best! You will draw up the tactics, morale strategies. You know, you know the gaps, the weaknesses... Let me show you off to your new comrades. Welcome! A better friend even than a good enemy. Oh, Marcius, this is a great, great thing that has happened. Give me your hand!

(*They go out, arms round one another.*)

FIRST MAN: I don't see this at all.

SECOND MAN: Nor I. Still, he's a rare man.

FIRST MAN: He is. But Aufidius is worth six of him.

SECOND MAN: Who can tell?

FIRST MAN: We'll see.

(*Enter THIRD MAN.*)

THIRD MAN: I don't like it. He's got them all in there listening to him – and Aufidius in the middle, like the rest. He's more hopping mad than *we* ever were.

SECOND MAN: Then we shall have the 'old times' stirring again. Let's get on with it, I say. Fighting's better than this sitting around. A fine campaign *this*. Action is move and muscle, peace is just lethargy and drowsy blood. Nothing to do but make unwanted babies in some strange place.

THIRD MAN: Perhaps we'll see the Romans done like they did the Volscians. Here's to it. We're coming. Good comrades!

(*They dash out.*)

Scene 5

Rome. Conference room. SICINIUS and BRUTUS.

SICINIUS: There's no news of him and I don't expect any.
Mark 'rendered harmless'. Everything's settled back into
the old ways so quickly. His old friends are quite put out
by it all. They'd rather have had the place in turmoil
even if it cost them money *and* what they own; and we
all know how much that means to 'em. Apparently,
happy workers make them feel more uneasy than
unfriendly ones.

BRUTUS: We had our show-down at the right time.
(*Enter MENENIUS.*)
Well, and here's Menenius to prove it.

SICINIUS: Indeed. Oh, he's got *very* friendly lately…
Hallo to you, sir.

MENENIUS: Hallo.

SICINIUS: Your Coriolanus doesn't seem missed
much except by a few friends. We seem to survive
without him. I wonder what he would think if he
were here.

MENENIUS: It certainly seems to have settled down. But
how much better it could have been if he could have
only yielded here and there.

SICINIUS: Have you heard where he is?

MENENIUS: No, I hear nothing. His wife and mother have
heard nothing either.

BRUTUS: Caius Marcius was good at what he was most
good at. War and just, oh, general hostility. But, added to
that, he was, let's see: insolent, overcome with pride,
ambitious beyond all thinking, self-loving –

SICINIUS: Aiming for himself and one self alone. Even
without support.

MENINIUS: I think that's an unfair assessment.

SICINIUS: You'd have soon found it so if he had ever
become consul.

BRUTUS: I think we can say we did well to prevent that
and Rome can sleep safely without him.

(*Enter MESSENGER with papers which he hands to MENENIUS.*)

MENENIUS: (*Reading.*) It's Aufidius. Just what I feared. With Marcius gone, he's come out of his hole as I knew he would.

SICINIUS: Marcius? Aufidius? This is all rumour. The Volscians wouldn't dare take us on again.

MENENIUS: Can't be! We know very well that it *can.* Three times it's happened in my own lifetime.

BRUTUS: It's not possible.

MESSENGER: More news is coming in all the time. No one knows quite what's happening or what to do. It's being said openly, how probable I don't know, that Marcius has joined up with Aufidius; they've joined up together against Rome and planned such horrors beyond – well, contemplation.

SICINIUS: This makes sense.

BRUTUS: Thinking that the weakest ones among us will welcome Marcius back again on any terms...

SICINIUS: Exactly.

MENENIUS: I don't believe it. He and Aufidius are too much for each other.

(*Enter COMINIUS.*)

COMINIUS: You must go to the Senate at once. An incredible force led by, yes, Caius Marcius and Aufidius with him has landed already and is hurtling at this moment towards the city and with hardly any resistance from us. Oh, you have done well, I hope you are pleased with yourselves. The place will fall on your heads and the rest of us with you. Oh, you have done well, believe me.

MENENIUS: And this is true about Marcius and the Volscians?

COMINIUS: He's like a *god* to them. He leads them against us like something out of hell, only better. They chase us like schoolboys after butterflies which is all we are, according to their book.

MENENIUS: Well, you *have* all done well, you and your fighting workers, you revolutionaries, you brawny slogan-turners. What about you now then?

COMINIUS: He'll shake Rome about your ears.

BRUTUS: Is this really true?

COMINIUS: I promise you, you won't find out otherwise, anywhere. Everything is going down in front of him. And who can blame him? Your *enemies* have found something in him.

MENENIUS: We're finished unless he chooses otherwise.

COMINIUS: And who shall ask for it? The Tribunes can't. They've no real power. They've been shown up for what they are. Even if his best friend should say, please be good to Rome, you think they would get a show of less hatred now?

MENENIUS: You are right. If he were setting fire to my own house I wouldn't have the face to say, please don't. You've done well, you've done well, as you meant to do from the beginning.

COMINIUS: (*To Tribunes.*) What you've brought on Rome! Even our worst times were never so terrible as this. And helpless.

BRUTUS/SICINIUS: No, not us... (*Etc.*)

MENENIUS: Then who was it? Are you saying it was *us*? We loved him for what he was and could have been, but like the miserable beasts we are, we gave in to your mob and let them hoot him out of the city.

COMINIUS: But I think you'll find they'll roar him in again. Tullus Aufidius, ah – only just less a personality than Coriolanus, takes his cue as if he were some mere assistant. And against all this, we have – what? (*MENENIUS looks out of the window.*)

MENENIUS: Here they come. Here come the mobs now. Aufidius? With Coriolanus? You are the ones who howled and voted for the exiling of him. Now he's coming back with his own army and as many of you will yell out 'welcome back' as hurled him out. Never mind. If he could burn us, every one of us, like a huge coal in the universe, we'd deserve it. You're good things, you and your voices. You've done well with them with your linked arms and trying to storm the Capitol. And *we* let you do it!

COMINIUS: Oh yes, what else?

(*COMINIUS and MENENIUS go out accompanied by the MESSENGER.*)

BRUTUS: I don't like this.

SICINIUS: Nor I.

BRUTUS: Let's go to the Capitol. I'd give everything I have if this were just rumour.

SICINIUS: I don't think it is. Let's go.

(*They go out.*)

Scene 6

Enter AUFIDIUS with one of his lieutenants.

AUFIDIUS: They still flock to that Roman.

LIEUTENANT: I don't know what it is about him but our men use his name like saying grace before a meal. This is not good for you... that your own men –

AUFIDIUS: I can't help it now. It's too early to take steps. Certainly he's taken wing. Even to me, more than I thought he would when we first clutched each other but he's the self same man. One must excuse what can't be changed – while it suits.

LIEUTENANT: I still wish, sir – I mean for your own sake – that you'd not gone into double harness. Perhaps it would have been better to have done the whole thing yourself or even to have let him get on with it on his own.

AUFIDIUS: I know what you mean well enough. But you can be sure of that, that when his account comes in, he has no idea of what *I* can charge against him. Oh, I will agree with you that to the Volscian state he does seem a brilliant manager, does all he can and leaves no possibility unexamined; and up till now, he has done what was promised. Still, something will be left undone and that will either break his neck or mine, when we come to the adding up.

LIEUTENANT: Do you think, sir, that he'll take Rome on his own? Everywhere's surrendering to him before he

starts. The nobility of Rome are in his pocket; so too are
the Senators and Patricians. As for the Tribunes, no
soldiers they and as for the people, they'll be as keen to
mark their yeses in the right place as they were to mark
'no' before.

AUFIDIUS: Oh, I think he'll be to Rome what a piranha
is to an over-fleshed human. It's the nature of them
both, as he was their honoured servant but then couldn't
keep his balance. Whether it was pride brought on by
unbroken boyish fame, who knows, but he was lucky in
it, whatever it was it may have been. Perhaps he had
defective judgment in following up; certainly he had
the chances. But whatever, this was a right royal rising
up of one man we've not seen the like of – not in our
time; at any rate. But even in all this he was feared and
hated more than *anybody*. Can you think of anyone else
it was like? Everything he had going for him – it was
quite enough to gag on and eventually choke. So
whatever value any one of us may have is: no more
than what the time puts on to it, and power, however
comfortable for its run to sit in, is a pretty hard coffin
to lie in. One fire drives out one fire; one nail one nail;
rights foundered by rights; strength by strength; they
all fail. Let's go. When Caius, Rome is yours, you will
never have been so poor, for I think then you might
belong to me.

Scene 7

*Rome. Conference room. MENENIUS, COMINIUS, SICINIUS
and BRUTUS.*

MENENIUS: No, I'll not go to see him. You have heard
what he said about me; I was once his commander.
I loved him in a most, a most particular way. He called
me his father once, but – so what now? You go, you that
got rid of him. Kneel down before his headquarters and
crawl your way back into his mercy if you can. No, if he
was reluctant to listen to Cominius, I'll stay at home.

COMINIUS: He didn't want to know me.

MENENIUS: You hear that?

COMINIUS: He did call me by my first name once.
I turned on the times we've had together, the good ones
and the bloody ones. Coriolanus: he wouldn't answer to
that name. In fact, no names. He was a kind of nothing,
nameless; without title; until he had burned a new one
for himself out of Rome.

MENENIUS: Oh yes, you Tribunes, you've done your
work well. We shall make a good memorial.

COMINIUS: I tried reminding him how gracious it is for
someone like him to forgive but he said he would treat it
just like any other petition among the rest.

MENENIUS: What else did he say?

SICINIUS: I know this, that if you would go to him, you
could do more than any army we might have or any
politician.

MENENIUS: No.

SICINIUS: Please.

MENENIUS: To do what?

SICINIUS: Only you can save Rome from Marcius.

MENENIUS: Well, and what if Marcius sends me packing
like Cominius here, not even listened to – what then?
Just another late friend shot down with one of his
glances. What if that happens?

SICINIUS: Then you will have done all you can.

MENENIUS: Very well. I'll try. I think he *may* listen to
me. From Cominius's account, it may well be that he
was not approached at the right time, or mood or
something, not fed or overtired. I'll try and see to it
that the circumstances are a bit better this time. If
I think the time *is* right, I'll talk to him like the
old days.

BRUTUS: You know what a sort of maze his heart is but
you do at least know the way.

MENENIUS: I'll do my best with him. How it turns out is
another thing. I'll report as soon as I can.
(*Exit MENENIUS.*)

COMINIUS: He won't listen to him.

SICINIUS: Won't?

COMINIUS: I tell you he sits up to his ears in admiration; with blood in both eyes and nothing but Rome will catch either of them. There's no appealing to him. He just told me to go and sent me off without a word. No word after and nothing about what he would or wouldn't do. No discussions even, there *is* nothing left. Oh, there's his wife and mother. I believe they have plans for trying to reason with him but I don't set much store by that. However, we shall see.

(*They go out.*)

Scene 8

CORIOLANUS's headquarters in front of Rome. MENENIUS is under guard.

MENENIUS: You, you, listen to me.

(*Enter CORIOLANUS and AUFIDIUS.*)

CORIOLANUS: What's the matter?

MENENIUS: You see, you can't keep me from my own Coriolanus. (*To CORIOLANUS.*) Oh, my boy, my dear boy. What are you preparing for us? Look, I'm here to talk to you. I wasn't coming but then I was told there was only myself left. I've been blown out of Rome by petitions!

CORIOLANUS: Go away.

MENENIUS: What! Away!

CORIOLANUS: I no longer know you. Wife, mother, child, I wish to know nothing *of* you. My interests are in other places. Friends, family, lovers, we may have been, but that is past, so get along with you. My deafness is more powerful than *your* voice, I promise you. You'll have a safe conduct, I shall see to that. Otherwise, I want to hear nothing from you, you understand, *nothing.* This man Aufidius is my comrade. Look at him, and remember it. You see, Aufidius?

AUFIDIUS: Oh, you are loyal.

(*The GUARDS hustle out MENENIUS with their automatics. CORIOLANUS and AUFIDIUS sit down.*)

CORIOLANUS: Tomorrow Rome itself, his own home, will be bombarded. My good friend, I hope you'll tell your Volscians how I've dealt with these people.

AUFIDIUS: You have been impeccable.

CORIOLANUS: This last old man; it was not easy sending him back to Rome; he always held me up like a son to him. He was their last resource. Well, after him, no more, from state or friends or anybody.

(*There is a noise from outside.*)

I suppose that's one more delegation trying to racket its way in. Well, that's the last.

(*Enter VIRGILIA, VOLUMNIA and YOUNG MARCIUS.*)

(*To AUFIDIUS.*) It's Virgilia. And my mother and the boy. Well, enough of that. Oh, my mother bows, does she? Now that she wants something that can't be given. Even my young boy's put on a face which he thinks can't be denied. Let the Volscians plough up Rome and harrow all Italy: I'll never be such a moulting animal as to give in to instinct; but stand up here as if a man were creator of himself; and knew no other family or friend…

VIRGILIA: My dearest.

CORIOLANUS: These are not the same eyes you saw last time in Rome.

VIRGILIA: Seeing us here in this way makes you say this.

CORIOLANUS: Like a played out actor I've forgotten my lines. Forgive me, but don't ask me in return to forgive our Romans. God, I babble on just at the sight of two women.

VOLUMNIA: It's we who ask your forgiveness.

CORIOLANUS: What's this? You ask me?

VOLUMNIA: Your son, your wife, myself, we all do.

CORIOLANUS: Stop. Don't put this display on for me. You vulgarise yourselves. Don't ask me to give up my army or make terms with Rome, Rome's workers. Don't tell me I'm unnatural. Above all, don't reason with me.

VOLUMNIA: Oh, no more, no *more*. You've said you won't give us anything. All we've already asked is denied. But we still ask all the same. Even if it does do no more than harden your outline for the world to make sure. So listen to us.

CORIOLANUS: Aufidius and all you other Volscians, listen. Mark for yourselves: for I hear nothing from Rome that's in private. (*To VOLUMNIA.*) Well?

VOLUMNIA: Would you seriously have us look on silently and watch the husband, son, the father, tear his country's bowels out! For myself, son, I don't intend to wait to see the outcome of this war. If I can't persuade you to your own natural good grace, then trample on me first.

VIRGILIA: Yes, and me too, and this boy. So much for keeping your name.

YOUNG MARCIUS: He won't trample on me. I'll run away and then when I'm bigger, I'll go back and fight him. (*CORIOLANUS clutches MARCIUS's shoulders.*)

CORIOLANUS: It is not necessary for me to see any of you. I have sat here too long.

VOLUMNIA: No, don't go in this way. You know, my son, the general, the end of any war's uncertain, but this much is certain, that if you do overcome Rome, there will be no name like Coriolanus written in it for *you*. All that will be said is fine he may have been but his last expedition was no less of a ruin than his own country. Think of a name for that! Have you nothing to say? Do you think it a good thing for a man like yourself only to remember wrong? Virgilia, speak to him. Your crying means *nothing* to him. Speak up, boy: perhaps your tears can move him a bit more than we can. He lets me stand in front of him like a beggar. You have never shown your mother any courtesy, or perhaps *this* is it. When all she's thought of is what you have done and what you are and how you shall be. Your glory has been all I've lived for. Say what I ask for is not proper and then turn me back; then, then you can call yourself honest. Look at him, he can't even look at me, he turns away… The name of Coriolanus means more to him than ours; so this is the end. We will get back to Rome, and I with the rest of them. This boy doesn't know what he's asking for but you'd refuse him everything. Come, Virgilia. This man's mother must have been a Volscian, his wife is in Corioli and his child no more than a stand-up chance. Tell us to go. I shall say nothing until our city's under fire. Then – then, I'll have things to say!

(*CORIOLANUS holds his mother by the hand, silent.*)

CORIOLANUS: Oh, Mother, Mother! What have you done? Look, everyone watches this scene and laughs at every single element in it. Oh Mother, Mother! Oh! You've won a skilful victory for Rome, but, for your son, believe it, oh, believe it! – you don't know what you've done to *him*. But perhaps you do, and you were right to have done it. So be it…

(*To AUFIDIUS.*) Aufidius, though I can't make war too well, I can patch up the peace. Tell me, Aufidius, in my place, would you have done less? Or granted less? Aufidius?

AUFIDIUS: I'm most touched. (*He sounds cold.*)

CORIOLANUS: I dare say. It was no small thing to win me over but you will advise me. I know – I won't go to Rome. I'll stay here with you. We can stick together. Oh, Mother! Virgilia! Soon we will all have a drink together and we'll think about *other* things. We shall not after all be gone forever, in spite of what's happened. Come and have something to eat and drink with us, both of you. You deserve a shrine built to you; all the fire power in Italy and the entire world could not have made this peace…

(*They go out.*)

Scene 9

Rome. Conference room. MENENIUS and SICINIUS. Enter high-ranking POLICE OFFICER.

POLICE OFFICER: Sir, I would advise you both to return home while you can. Sicinius, madam, the Plebians have got your fellow tribune and hung him upside down. If

Marcius's ladies don't come back with something, things are going to be very bad indeed. He's dying by inches at this moment.

(*Enter another POLICE OFFICER.*)

SICINIUS: Well?

SECOND POLICE OFFICER: The news looks good after all. The ladies seem to have had their way. The Volscians are moving out now, already. There's no Marcius! Rome's even starting to look a bit like its old self!

SICINIUS: Is this true? Are you certain?

SECOND POLICE OFFICER: As certain as one can be, madam. Listen!

(*Sounds of celebration outside.*)

MENENIUS: I'll go and meet Volumnia and the wife. They are worth all of this, this city, full of politicians like myself, yes and tribunes. They must have a real welcome.

(*They go. Noise of celebration grows.*)

Scene 10

Corioli. AUFIDIUS's headquarters. AUFIDIUS with LIEUTENANTS.

AUFIDIUS: Get the others in here. It's him I accuse. Now! Move.

(*Exit LIEUTENANT, to be followed by several more entering.*)

Come in.

FIRST LIEUTENANT: And how's our general?

AUFIDIUS: Feeling like any man betrayed feels.

SECOND LIEUTENANT: The people must know where they are, where they stand, where *you* stand.

AUFIDIUS: I know. I gambled and I gambled and I gambled! I seem to be his follower to every one, not partner. It was as if I'd been a mercenary to a mercenary.

FIRST LIEUTENANT: It had to be admitted some time. We all marvelled at it. And at the very end when we had got Rome itself and everything was open to us –

AUFIDIUS: That was it. How could I be so weak! Just for a few tears. I've seen enough. They can be as cheap as lies. He sold out without an hour's labour. Well, he shall get the reward. Listen!

(*Outside drums, trumpets and shouts.*)

FIRST LIEUTENANT: You slunk into your own time like a nobody and he comes home the conquering hero.

SECOND LIEUTENANT: Do what you feel. We all feel it.

AUFIDIUS: Say no more. Here are the others.

(*Enter various other OFFICIALS of the Volscian Army.*)

OFFICIALS: Welcome back.

AUFIDIUS: I don't deserve welcome. Do you know what's happened?

OFFICIALS: We do.

FIRST OFFICIAL: There has been a terrible yielding here – and there's no excuse for it.

AUFIDIUS: Here he comes. Hear him for yourself.

(*Enter CORIOLANUS, accompanied by drum and colours.*)

CORIOLANUS: My friends! I've come back *and* I'm still one of you. Still unseduced, unseduced by my past loves as when I left you still under your command... As you know, I got us to the gates of Rome itself. We have brought back all kinds of concessions, more than I could ever have hoped for and we've made peace; peace with honour to *us* and what is nothing more than shame to the Romans! See what I've brought back!

(*He makes to hand to them a document.*)

AUFIDIUS: Don't read it, my friends. Don't bother to read it. Just tell the traitor how he's abused you all.

CORIOLANUS: Traitor! What's this!

AUFIDIUS: Yes, traitor, Marcius!

CORIOLANUS: Marcius!

AUFIDIUS: Yes, Marcius, Caius Marcius. Do you think I'll let you get away with that name you pilfered, Coriolanus, in Corioli?

CORIOLANUS: You're a true patriot, Aufidius, for a true patriot is a good hater. You come from a good-natured people and you have many virtues but they are of the

heart, a cold one too, not of the head. In your passions
and affections you are sincere but in understanding;
you are all hypocrites, every one. When you begin
to calculate the consequences, self-interest prevails
over everything. You have wit, genius, eloquence,
imagination, affection: but you have no understanding
and consequently no standard of thought or action.
Your strength of mind cannot keep up with the pace of
your so-called warmth of feeling Or your apparent
quickness. Your animal spirits run away with you. Oh
yes, there is something crude and undigested and
discordant in almost everything you do *or* say. You have
no system, no abstract ideas. You are everything by
starts, and nothing long. You are a wild lot. You hate
any law that imposes on your understanding or any
kind of restraint at all. You are all fierceness and levity.
If you have any feelings, when they aren't excited by
novelty or opposition, they grow cold and stagnant. If
your blood's not heated by passion, then it turns to
poison.

AUFIDIUS: I saw him, I watched him like a twist of rotten
silk. He whined and roared away your victory! We all
blush to look at him.

CORIOLANUS: Dear God, do you hear this!

AUFIDIUS: Don't bring in God, you boy of tears.

CORIOLANUS: Ha!

AUFIDIUS: No more.

CORIOLANUS: You penurious liar... You've made my
heart too big! 'Boy!' Oh, you *servant.* Forgive me – this is
the first time ever – what you see now must give this
churlish bitch the lie.

ALL: Cool down, both of you. Let's talk. (*Etc.*)

CORIOLANUS: Cut me to pieces, Volscians. Men, and
men like children. 'Boy'! You filth in my own place. Yes,
me. I was like an eagle in your dovecote. I fluttered your
precious Volscians in Corioli! Alone... I did it. 'Boy'?

AUFIDIUS: You see!

ALL: Kill him! Put it in! Get on with it! (*Etc.*)

(*They all close in on him.*)

CORIOLANUS: Oh, that I had him. With six Aufidiuses and more – his whole tribe. I'd have them ALL!
(*AUFIDIUS howls like a dog and everyone advances on CORIOLANUS who is quickly overwhelmed and disappears under the weight of his colours. Presently they all stand back and look upon the body.*)

AUFIDIUS: My friends, you cannot know even in this rage what he did to me, let alone to you. You should be glad he's gone. Even so, he was like some of us, unable to forgive wrongs when they seemed to darken death or night, to defy power, which seems omnipotent...neither to change, nor falter, nor repent even this...this to him was to be good, great and joyous, beautiful and from this alone, yes, life, joy, empire and victory.

LIEUTENANT: Well, let's make the best of it.

AUFIDIUS: (*Looking up.*) Take him up. Help me, three of you; I'll be one.
(*Sound of a helicopter. Four ropes attached to a stretcher descend from above the proscenium arch.*)

AUFIDIUS: He widowed and unchilded many a one in this city and we're the poorer for it. Still someone may remember. Help me.
(*AUFIDIUS and three LIEUTENANTS lay the body of CORIOLANUS onto the stretcher and cover it with a blanket. It ascends slowly and they watch it and then go out. All that remains on the stage is the lone figure of a piper playing a lament.*)

The End.